To Stir the Soul

To Stir the Soul
Spiritual Inspirations from Notre Dame

Jim Langford

To Stir the Soul
Spiritual Inspirations from Notre Dame

10 9 8 7 6 5 4 3 2

ISBN: 978-1-7321150-6-4

Published by
CORBY BOOKS
P.O. Box 93
Notre Dame, IN 46556
corbybooks.com

Manufactured in the United States of America

Dedicated To

Foreword

St. John Bosco, more commonly known as Don Bosco, founded the Salesians of Don Bosco, and with the help of St. Mary Mazzarello, he also founded the Salesian Sisters, the Daughters of Mary Help of Christians. One of the many gifts that he gave these religious communities is what is called the "good night." Prior to retiring in each house, each evening, the Superior gives the "good night" to the community. The "good night" is a brief talk that hopes to inspire, console, challenge, and animate the community in their walk with God. The "good night" is something that the community can think about, can reflect on, and can bring to bed with them. It is a beautiful and helpful practice in Salesian life.

In his latest book *To Stir the Soul*, Jim Langford has provided us with a book of magnificent and beautiful and lovely "good nights." Jim brings together stories and reflections and poems and writings from many people, of different faiths, men and women, living and deceased. Some are well known while others are not so. Jim divides these reflections into the most important topics in this world—faith, hope, love, death, and life.

Some of the reflections will make you smile and chuckle. Some of the stories will make you cry and sob. Some of the writings will make you think that the author has been inside of your soul and is talking about you. Some will make you stop and open your eyes and become aware of a reality you never thought about. These reflections are guaranteed to inspire the reader.

As I read the manuscript I found myself consoled again and again by the mercy of God, challenged by my first-world living and acting, inspired by the story of a father who learns that his son died while climbing a mountain. Some of the reflections talk about places on the campus of Notre Dame. If the reader is at Notre Dame, he/she will feel drawn to go to the Grotto and read the reflections while sitting at the Grotto. The reader will want to go for a walk on God quad on a quiet morning and read Father Ayo's reflection about God quad.

Many of the entries are from Holy Cross priests. As a Holy Cross priest, I felt a special gratitude to God for sending such wonderful and talented men to be my brothers in Holy Cross. (I got in when no one was watching the door!)

Several of the best entries are from the author himself, from other books that Jim has written. It's clear that Jim has spent a life time marinating in faith and hope and love and death and life.

I wholeheartedly recommend this book. The reader will not be disappointed. On the contrary the reader will find himself/herself inspired, consoled, challenged, and animated in their walk with God. *To Stir the Soul* is a wonderful and beautiful collection of "good nights."

Fr. Joe Corpora, C.S.C.

Acknowledgments

I want to thank the authors of all the pieces collected here, especially the members of the Congregation of Holy Cross whose words grace these pages.

I owe Tim Carroll of Corby Books, a man of many talents and longtime close friend, a debt of endless thanks for his encouragement and work seeing this book through the publishing process.

Preface

My career in book publishing is more than 50 years old. I have been an acquisitions editor at Doubleday in New York, Executive Editor at the University of Michigan Press, Director of the University of Notre Dame Press for 25 years, consultant at Rowman and Littlefield, and co-publisher at Corby Books. I have had a hand in publishing more than 1,000 books.

To Stir the Soul pretty much wrote itself. It draws almost completely on books I have helped publish and, to be honest, re-reading, selecting, and bringing them together has truly stirred my own soul.

These pieces offer wonderful food for meditation and action about things that really matter in life. On behalf of the authors gathered here, I offer them to all who may experience a rejuvenation of spirit. May this book brighten your soul as it has mine.

Jim Langford

Table of Contents

FAITH

"Cultivate a genuine faith. You will struggle with doubts and questions, but that is all part of developing a true faith. Blase Pascal said that in faith there is enough light for those who want to believe and enough shadow to blind those who don't. That's why it is faith. I have found that it is precisely struggling through the doubts and questions that has deepened my faith. In moments of darkness and doubt, pray for faith. Make time for prayerful silence in your life."

—Fr. John Jenkins C.S.C.,
A Letter to My Freshman Self, vol. 2, 2.

THIS IS A POEM written by Terry Anderson, the Associated Press reporter who was on assignment in the Middle East and was taken hostage by radical Shiite Muslims in Beirut, Lebanon, and who survived nearly seven years in captivity. He titles it:

"FAITH"

"Where is faith found
Not in a book
or in a church,
not often or
for everyone.
In childish times
it's easier;
a child believes
just what it's told.
But children grow
and soon begin
to see too much
that doesn't match
the simple tales,
and not enough

of what's behind
their parents' words.
There is no God,
the cynics say;
We made Him up
out of our need
and fear of death.
And happily they offer up
their test-tube proofs.
A mystery,
the priests all say,
and point to saints
who prove their faith
in acts of love
and sacrifice.
But what of us
who are not saints
only common
human sinners?
And what of those
who in their need
and pain cry out
to God and go
on suffering?
I do not know—

I wish I did.
Some times I feel
all the world's pain
I only say
that once in my
own need I felt
a light and warm
and loving touch
that eased my soul
and banished doubt
and let me go on to the end.
It is not proof—
there can be none.
Faith's what you find
when you're alone
and find you're not."

—Terry Anderson, in *Den of Lions: Memoirs of Seven Years*,
cited in *Langford, God Moments*, 133-35.

"HERE IS SOMETHING YOU SHOULD KNOW: There is a God.

"Of course, you will spend a lifetime thinking, watching, looking, doubting, searching, questioning, believing, and then wondering again, thinking maybe so, it might be true, then losing track again, in the face of all the evidence to the contrary. And that's OK. That's how you talk to God, how you engage God in conversation. The constant back and forth, the restless desire to figure it all out, the purpose, the meaning, the battle between faith and reason, the heart and mind. It means you really care, that you really want to know. Keep on Him.

"But I can tell you, sitting here at 64, looking back, there is a God, by whatever name: Higher Power, Great Spirit, the Way, the Truth and the Life, The Force, hidden energies of the universe. He's really there, somehow. And I have seen Him at work. Right in my—your—very life. I won't tell you how. Life needs surprises. That's something else: A sense of humor is essential equipment for the trip.

"Life is kind of like, well, it's like many things, all kinds of analogies. But the one I like most right now is that life is like white-water rafting. It's a bumpy, thrilling, exciting, scary ride. And the currents are more in control of things than you, your little raft, and your paddle. The sooner you learn to enjoy the ride the better off you'll be. It won't always be easy. You'll get scared. The dangers up ahead will make you nervous and afraid in anticipation. But try to remember that the apprehension over expectations is always worse than the experience itself. Read the currents.

"And get good people in the raft with you—people who can laugh, or at least smile back when the going gets tough, people who stand by you when it gets rough, who pull you through the tight spots. And a few scouts help, too. Some wise and friendly folks who can show you things. I know you like your solitude, that you like going your own way, doing it your way. Being comfortable in your own skin, alone with yourself, is a very good thing.

"But people will enrich your life if you let them. Of course, they will also break your heart. But that means you felt and felt deeply, loved a lot. Loved strong. And that's really good, because the most important thing we do in life is love. Everything else is secondary. Everything else you want, all your goals, your wealth, your awards, and your professional achievements . . . all less important than how well you loved.

"Here's the other very important thing. Happiness. Find true happiness, not the fleeting kind. Or things and times that bring temporary happiness. But the happiness that comes with love and being loved, fulfillment and peace. Live with gratitude; happiness follows.

"You might also be interested to know that a lot of things you now know are the very things you should remember throughout your lifetime. All those ideals and principles, the truths and stones of wisdom and goodness—hold onto them, even as life wears them away, hides and steals them, sells you false treasures. It is true what they say about the temporal and eternal, the seen and unseen. Don't let go of the treasures you cannot see. Stay true to the ideals of your youth, and don't be so afraid. So reticent and timid. Don't care so much what other people think. Listen to 35 me, aye. I have gotten less bold, less adventurous as the years have gone by. Safer, more cautious. Don't lose courage and daring as the years go by. Be more like you and less like me.

"Stay on course, though, and follow the path of your heart's desire, the one you set out upon as a teenager, when that great door opened to you. The Way, the Tao, the soul of all creation. And those things you sometimes think are signs, and then wonder if they are signs, or if you are imagining them as signs? They are signs. They will be your guideposts, your mile markers, your trail posts. Pay attention to them. "*Mitakuye iyasin!*" the Lakota say. "All my relations." And listen to your heart. It knows things your brain can't catch up to. Trust it. That's where God lives, in all of that. Stay close to all He made.

"These may all seem like grand and cosmic themes. Pretentious perhaps; certainly squishy. You probably want more practical advice, windows to the future. So here: In your life's work you will stay in the minor leagues, but that's OK. You will get to play the game throughout your life. Few people are as privileged and blessed as those whose life's work is such sport. And whose life's work is somehow dedicated to something bigger than themselves. You'll find fatherhood is good beyond measure—though it brings its share of sacrifice and worry. Still, you'll get the better end of all the tradeoffs. Life is all about tradeoffs. Oh, and you and your parents will grow closer in time; the divides will come down when you all live long enough to see.

"I think that's about it. Oh. Don't throw away your baseball cards, sing along with the songs you love, play basketball for as long as you can—it's good for your health and lots more fun than running. Don't ever stop being a kid. Read. Be a good friend. Keep exploring. And remember you will die someday.

"And so live accordingly. That's a pretty good calibration for the decisions you make, the things you seek, the roads you travel, how you spend your time on earth. It's OK to fear death; the idea is unnervingly strange and scary. But there is a God; His wonders and gifts have shown me so. You will get them, too, in time. Meanwhile, be an attentive passenger in His creation.

—Kerry Temple, in *Letter to My Freshman Self*, vol. 1, 61-64.

"RELIGION IS NOT ONLY CREED, not only church, not only cult; religion is also *faith*. This element of faith probably has been subject to more misunderstanding than any other element of the religious life. Many people have supposed that religious faith means that their religion can be used by them as a crutch, a cure-all, a way of healing physical illness, becoming successful in one's work, or coping with human relations in the family, on the job, or elsewhere. But authentic religious life in all cultures and all faiths is something that comes out of the fulness of a person's heart. It is a gift in which we express your love, rather than something which comes out of the poverty of our lives as a demand that something be given to us.

"All religion, no doubt, is rooted in the dark night of the soul in which we must wrestle with an angel against the doubts and despair into which we are plunged by a sense of our mortality, by a sense of our alienation from the world, and by a sense of our finitude, our limitations. In all of the major religions, faith has not meant a capacity to believe propositions without evidence, or in the face of the evidence; faith has not had to do with evidence. It has meant, rather, a capacity to commit ourselves, to entrust ourselves, to affirm the meaning and value of life, whatever the problems with which we are beset. What is fundamental in faith is an attitude of humility, of knowing our limitations as human beings, and an attitude of appreciation of life, affirmation of life, gratitude for life.

"...Religion can be a matter of dependencies, but it can also be a matter of humility. It can express anxiety, but also trust. It can manifest guilt, but also moral responsibility. It can invite a life of fantasy, but it can also bring to a focus and provide a channel for expression of our joy in God's world."

—Abraham Kaplan, in *Love...and Death,* 25-26.

"UNLIKE IN THE MODERN ERA, the question today is not so much about proving God's existence as it is about experiencing God's existence. Theologians range from those who argue for a pre-modern understanding of God that exempts all talk of God from contemporary scientific and intellectual scrutiny, to those who embrace the pluralism and diversity of the day to the point of not talking about God at all. Somewhere in between, theologians put God in conversation with the culture without baptizing the culture or compromising revelation or tradition.

"I fall into this middle road.

"All my life I have struggled to reconcile faith in God with the world I see and experience. For reasons that belong to the realm of mystery, the moments of clarity, in which God's presence is obvious to me, come and go. Like a cosmic game of hide-and-go-seek, now I see God, now I don't. Sometimes I find God right where I figured I would—in long conversations with close friends, at the dinner table with family, in hugs from loved ones, at weddings, funerals, and baptisms. Other times I am surprised to find God, as Catholic novelist Flannery O'Connor once wrote, "flitting from tree to tree in the back of our minds," calling me to look more deeply into who I am, daring me to drop my baggage and run free. And sometimes God finds me just when I least expect it, when I have turned my back and given up.

"None of us can describe God, exactly, but we know when we have God moments. We know it in our souls. They are moments of recognition when we know what is true, realize what is real, and experience what is good. God moments are rare glimpses into eternity that happen in time. They are moments pregnant with love and life that help us give birth to our best selves and encourage others to find their best selves. They are moments that fill us with thanksgiving, overwhelm us with joy, offer us hope, and transforms a moment in time (*chronos*) into a sacred moment (*chairos*) that fuels our journey. They are moments that teach us that faith really matters, that the stories of God's creation and ongoing love always exist, even if we put them on the cutting room floor in a world of soundbites and shattered meaning.

"The trouble with God moments is that we forget them so easily. We go right back to playing hide-and-go seek with God. Sometimes God hides and we find her. Sometimes we hide and he finds us. But the eternal question: "Where in the world is God?" echoes in the marrow of our bones."

—Jeremy Langford, "Where in the Postmodern World is God? in *Walking With God in a Fragile World*, 96-97.

"WHEN I DOUBT my convictions or forget that Jesus and Christianity embrace seekers, I turn to the Bible to remind myself that I am not alone in asking questions and that, no matter what, I am loved. For these reasons, one of my favorite Bible stories is John 1:35–38 in which Jesus asks two curious men following him, "What do you seek?" and invites them to 'Come and See.' In those few words Jesus asks the great question and extends the great invitation of Christianity. By asking, 'What do you seek?' Jesus is also asking, 'Who are you?' 'Where are you going?' 'How will you get there?' The great promise of Christianity is that in asking we receive, in knocking we gain entrance, and in seeking we find. The religious rub here is that in holding Christianity to its promise, we are held to asking questions, thinking about why we are here, celebrating the solidarity of all creation, loving and forgiving others, working for peace and justice. These are not actions only for religious people. They are for anyone seeking to live more deeply. To help us live more deeply, Jesus invites us to come and see. Seeing with the eyes of faith is never easy—Jesus' own disciples struggled mightily and, even after seeing all he had shown them, did not know what to make of the empty tomb and did not recognize the resurrected Jesus until he gave them a sign. In today's fast-paced world, we squint to make sense of the blurs streaming past our faces.

"Meaning changes, eluding our grasp. Knowledge is revised and supplanted by yet more knowledge. Truths come and go. Gurus and self-proclaimed prophets have their moments and fade into the distance. But, as with the dejected disciples on the road to Emmaus, Jesus walks with us until we have eyes to see and ears to hear. Throughout his ministry, Jesus healed those who lived physically and metaphorically in the darkness. But he did more than help them see in a human way; he shared his light with them so that they could see who he was and who they could become. Time and again Jesus shows us that believing and seeing are paths to each other—seeing leads to believing, but, more importantly in this age, believing leads to seeing. He also shows us that seeing with the eyes of faith is often a gradual process and that, when we come to see with the eyes of faith, the only proof of what we see is the way we live and love."

—Jeremy Langford, "Where in the Postmodern World is God" in *Walking with God in a Fragile World*, 100-01.

A Story Of Faith

"...A MOUNTAIN CLIMBER was high on a mountain and he fell. Fortunately, he grabbed a bush growing out of the mountainside and hung there with his feet dandling in space, hundreds of feet above ground He called out to his friend but the friend couldn't get to him.

"He then called out to anyone above for help 'Is there anyone up there?' A voice from above answered, 'I am here' 'Who are you?' said the climber. 'I am God'. came the answer. The man was overjoyed and asked for help. God said 'I will help you, but first you have to do what I tell you.' 'Anything, anything at all,' replied the climber. Then God said, 'Let go of the bush.' There was a long silence from the climber, then he looked up and yelled, 'Is there anyone else up there?'

"That story says a lot about faith. We find faith tough. By it God seems frequently to demand the impossible. He keeps saying, 'Let go of the bush.'...

"It would be bad enough, albeit a lot easier, if it were just a matter of being hung up with that bush once, if we just had to let go in trust one time. But we know better. Faith demands that we let go frequently; it means abandoning our blueprint; it means living in the midst of ambiguity and doubt.

"Faith is a wild risk...the faith experience, the constant call to let go, will involve our willingness to leave the known and familiar for what is sometimes threatening and insecure. The doubts that will come along will cost us, but the transformation is worth the pain. Reflecting on the growth occasioned by doubt in his own life, Dostoevsky once exclaimed "My hosannas were forged in the crucible of doubt."

"...Letting go of safety and security-at-any-price will make us vulnerable. It will lead us into waters uncharted except by faith. It will call us to take part in an exodus, sharing the lifestyle of those others who ventured into the unknown. Like a man named Abraham and another they called the Nazarene."

—Fr. William Toohey, C.S.C., in *Life After Birth*, 57-59.

WHENEVER WE SAY 'YES' to a project, a new value, a principle, a career decision, or to another person in friendship, we know it is going to cost us something. And this will be like a dying. But the death is really a putting to death of apathy, indifference, comfort, convenience, all those things which are obstacles to the pledge we've made."

—Fr. William Toohey C.S.C., in *Life After Birth*, 9.

" NOTRE DAME'S brilliant theologian, John Dunne, tells a fascinating story he calls 'The Parable of the Mountain.' In it he describes a man climbing a mountain at the top of which, he thinks, is God. By climbing the mountain and reaching God, he anticipates he will leave the pain of his shallow, empty life behind in the valley from which he has escaped. But while he climbs, God is coming down the mountain, down into the valley, down amidst the toil and grief. In the mists of the mountain, God and man pass one another.

"When the man reaches the mountain top he will find nothing. God is not there. What then will he do? He realizes his climb was a mistake. But what now? Agony and despair? Or will he turn to retrace his path, through the mists, into the valley, to where God had gone seeking him?

"Where God had gone seeking him"—this is the key. This is the very heart of the mystery of life. Religion, for example, is not so much our quest for God, but God's search for us. That is what it means to be a chosen people. Not that by some piety or accomplishment we have raised ourselves up over other people to a place of eminence, but that, in spite of our frailties and betrayals, God reaches out to choose us.

"We object. That's not our experience. Our experience is just the opposite. We are much more aware of *not* being chosen. In the midst of recalling how often we are not chosen, God would have us believe that He doesn't operate that way. He chooses each of us by name. We are each chosen first, and there are no conditions whatsoever. We find this hard to swallow. It's difficult to believe God would choose us, since we have so many experiences of not being chosen by anyone else—even ourselves.

"Of course, there is that strange man, Jesus, who was always choosing the 'unchoosable.' He constantly sought out the hurting, suffering, fearful, ordinary women and men, whose lives, more often than not, appeared futile and directionless.

"Take the good thief. I like to think that, in some way, he stands for each of us. He, too, had been running away from the pain of life, thinking that this was the way to find happiness. What a mess he had made of it...All the time the good thief had been searching for happiness, he didn't know that happiness had been looking for him. That's why the story of this bandit is the story of many of us. The quest for happiness (or the effort to escape from pain) is the quest for God. But He is the one who finds us first. That's why Christianity is good news. We don't pursue happiness, it pursues us."

—Fr. Bill Toohey C.S.C., in *Life After Birth*, 17-20.

Reaching out to the Hurting

"ALLOWING OURSELVES to get close to suffering and injustice can trigger pain, resistance, or anger in us. Christ up close is very human and sometimes uncomfortable. Yet our care for God's cherished children brings important blessings. We learn about inner life, about our hesitations and exclusiveness, about our personal and institutional limitations, about the need for grace and healing within us, our Church, and our world. Those hurting among us could lead us to pray that God might give us eyes to see, ears to hear, and a heart to understand real dignity—that is, Christ among us."

—Fr. Richard Berg, C.S.C., in *Fragments of Hope*, 106.

"THE GRATITUDE which is central to religious experience is beautifully exemplified in a very ancient Hebrew poem, the conclusion of which runs: 'To you alone, O God, we give thanks though our mouths were as full of song as the sea, though our tongues were as multitudinous as the waves and our lips of praise were as wide as the skies, though our eyes shone with light as the sun and the moon, though our hands were outspread as the eagles of heaven, though our feet were as swift as the deer: even then, we would still be unable to thank You, O God, our God, and the God of our fathers, for one thousandth, or one ten-thousandth part of what You have done for our fathers and for us. Therefore, the limbs which you have fashioned, the spirit which You have breathed into our nostrils, the tongue which you have set in our mouths, all these shall thank You, bless You, praise You, You, always You, only You. Whatever in me is high shall be made humble, whatever is brave shall be in awe, whatever is glad shall be grateful; and every part of your being shall sing Ha-lelu Yah: praised be God.'"

—Abraham Kaplan, in *Love...And Death*, 27.

"WHAT I HOPE TO DESCRIBE is a God worthy of belief and more than worthy. So much is at stake, If there is a loving God, who loved each and every one of us, really and truly, everything changes. The whole world has life and hope of eternal happiness; we are truly in the hands of an infinite God.

Finite god(s) would be no god(s)at all. If we conclude 'I cannot believe in God,' I hope at least it is with a sad sigh rather than with a 'thank God (scratch that) a 'thank goodness.' Everything is at stake if there is a God and what God is like. One can wait and see, and in fact we must all wait and see. Some anxiety and uncertainty will plague us all in our journey through life with, at best, a mysterious God. I want to say 'thank God,' for a God I could fully comprehend might not be much of a God."

—Fr. Nicholas Ayo, C.S.C. in *Your God May Be Too Small*, iv.

"No, GOD DOES NOT HIDE himself to make us search for him., of that I am sure,--much less to let us suffer to increase our merits, On the contrary, bent down over his creation which moves upwards to him, he works with all his power to give us happiness and light. Like a mother, he watches over his newly born child. But our eyes are unable to see him yet. Is not precisely the whole course of centuries needed in order for our gaze to accustom itself to the light?

"Our doubts, just as our sufferings, are the price and condition for the perfection of the universe. Under these conditions I consent to walk right to the end along a road of which I am more and more certain, towards an horizon, more and more shrouded in mist."

—Teilhard de Chardin, cited in *Teilhard de Chardin and the Mystery of Christ*, by Fr. Christopher F. Mooney, S.J., 155.

HOPE

"In the depths of winter,
I discovered there was in me
an invincible summer."

—Albert Camus

Unexpected Hope

"DISAPPOINTMENTS, reversals, sorrows, broken promises and defeats all challenge hopefulness. People say, "Well, I was hoping to find forgiveness in my heart or get over being sick... but, sadly, it wasn't to be. I've given up." People think miracles are few and far between. Actually miracles sneak up on us and take us by surprise. Finding hope itself may be almost like a miracle in these very difficult situations.

"Life sometimes deals tremendous blows, situations that cannot be changed. Chronic illnesses and permanent disabilities provide examples of the very difficult circumstances people face. Remarkably, despite the reality that no relief is possible, some people remain unexpectedly hopeful. This hope is a magnificent blessing that keeps people living often with extraordinary courage, acceptance and peace.

"In other situations, eventual healing may come but only after heartaches and long struggles, for example, success in achieving social justice during a life of helpless poverty, the unforeseen mending of broken friendships, finding freedom from addictions.

"One of the most hopeful passages in scripture is found in St. Paul's letter to the Romans. In his list of severe threats to life and happiness—afflictions, anguish, persecution, nakedness, famine, danger or the sword—Paul asks, "Who can separate us from the love of Christ?" He emphasizes that we are victorious in all these challenges through Christ who loves us. He continues by claiming that there is absolutely nothing in the world or beyond our world that can separate us from the love of God made visible in Christ Jesus our Lord.

To grasp this truth and live by it is true freedom achieved through hope. (author unknown)

A Story of Hope

"THERE'S MORE TO LIFE than what's going on here." She paused, tried for a better position in her chair and looked at me. 'Sister,' I responded, 'even here in our assisted living program you seem so able to see and live beyond all the suffering from your Parkinson's disease.' She nodded, and managed a smile. 'Twelve years ago, when I first learned of my Parkinson's, I was really scared and felt so confined by a terrible inner darkness. What an awful shock! My high school ministry would soon end. It took me some time to find the kind of hope that lets me tell you today there's more to this life than what's going on here.'

"Disabled and in physical pain, Sister Pat remains a hopeful activist while suffering: She tells me one of her mottoes: 'We suffer *for* something. Others are helped.' She and I talked about this since chronic suffering for so many has a way of pulling them into a lonely but somewhat bearable isolation. Sister related how she was eventually able to emerge from this solitary darkness as hope was kindled in her heart.

We spoke of the reality of the cross. Her cross is such a heavy one. Yet, Sister claims she is now more open than ever to the needs of the wider world. She knows that the cross is a fact of life and everywhere. The crucial issue is not that we have crosses but how well we manage them with God's help. Daily crosses may include difficulties with others or the distance of friends, lapses of health, loss of loved ones or property, personal failures, unfair treatment, seasons of loneliness or fatigue, bleakness in prayer, other hardships and what we have afflicted on others. Crosses are inevitable and unfriendly in everyone's life.

When you think about it, each small or large cross is an unwelcome visitor in our daily lives and lets us know, "You are not going to get your way." And so we remember that Jesus said, "If anyone wishes to come after me, he must deny himself and take up his cross daily and follow me."

That implies: If you wish to be my disciple, brace yourself. You will be prevented from getting your own way...daily... and for what purpose?

"The cross may help us identify with Jesus who gave his life on the cross for our salvation.

"Anticipating his crucifixion on the following day, Jesus prayed in the garden: 'My Father, if it is not possible that this cup pass without my drinking it, *your will be done!*' The disciples must have remembered the prayer the Lord taught them: 'your kingdom come, *your will be done*, on earth as in heaven.'

In the spiritual life, as we grow closer to God we learn the lessons of the cross. Our crosses seem to be teachers about selfishness and generosity, about self centeredness and humility. Reflecting back on our lives, we may become more aware that our crosses have indeed tamed our egos and allowed God's Spirit to bring the help of light, wisdom and strength.

"So often we want to hear, 'Have it your way.' Yes, have it my way. And then, in time, we learn to say to God, 'Have it Your way.' This is the challenging work of the cross, resulting in a special closeness with Christ who understands suffering and speaks to our soul: 'There's more to life than what's going on here.'

"As Pope Benedict XVI wrote in his encyclical on Christian hope, "When we attempt to avoid suffering by withdrawing from anything that might involve hurt, when we try to spare ourselves the effort and pain of pursuing the truth, love, and goodness, we drift into a life of emptiness, in which there may be almost no pain, but the dark sensation of meaninglessness and the abandonment is all the greater. It is not by sidestepping or fleeing from suffering that we are healed, but rather by our capacity for accepting it, maturing through it and finding meaning through union with Christ who suffered with infinite love.

"Hope is the virtue of seeing with confidence beyond the present moment, and even beyond the future, into the realm of eternal life with God."

—Fr.Richard Berg, C.S.C., in *Fragments of Hope*, 151.

"STORIES ARE 'FRAGMENTS.' As stories are remembered and pieced together, a larger picture or a life mosaic emerges. I think of my stories as pieces of a stained glass window, brightened by the light of God, reflecting hope. From childhood to older age these stories or fragments added shapes and colors to my hope. As people mature in faith and the love of God and neighbor, the virtue of hope empowers life for eternity.

"For the youngster, hope looks to the future. What is in store for me? I watch grownups with their friends. I might become like them. I watch and remember how they act. I think about what they say and how they deal with troubles. I notice good results and unfortunate ones. Older people have a way of setting my stage for life with hopefulness, courage and so much more. God may also enter my life in an unexpected and unforgettable way, drawing me into a mysterious friendship. My imagination may take God's invisible visitation in stride, probably not comprehending until later in life the impact of this friendship. But an intimate connection with God does unfold gradually with new clues about God's presence and love. In this way the fire of hope is kindled and will burn brighter."

—Fr. Richard F. Berg, C.S.C., in *Fragments of Hope*, 151.

Another Form of Hope

"SHE GLANCED OVER, nudged me and asked, 'If I may be so curious, what are you reading?' It was a book about funeral liturgies that I planned to finish on the plane before our arrival in Portland. Instead, we talked. 'I'm a widow. My husband died of cancer a few years ago and left me to raise our seven daughters. We planned for that, but he forgot to tell me about taking care of the car and his household repairs secrets.' I asked how she was managing. 'Well, Father, I found there's strength in remembering. So when I am stuck trying to solve a problem, I think of him and what he would do. You know, it works. It works for the girls, too. We are sure he's helping us.'

" 'Shortly before my own mother died, she told me she would like to help from heaven if she could. 'Years ago I read about St. Therese, the Little Flower, and her promise to bring good to the earth. You know, there may be something to that. Why can't all of us continue to help family and friends after we leave this life?'

"I thought of the Communion of Saints and our connections in the Body of Christ. 'Communications Central' must be the Holy Spirit of Christ, present here among us yet also dwelling beyond our world of space and time. And so, we have depended on our own Mother for help for the many years since she left us. Her heart always went out to members of our family who were sick or frail. We believe she and many others in God's keeping continue to assist us.' "

"An elderly widow named Virginia lived at Mary's Woods where I serve as their priest. She and her husband, Al, retired there several years ago. Al served as an attorney for a major railroad and Virginia was an accomplished ballerina. In their middle nineties their love and affection for one another continued to be tangible, real proof of their blessed years together and the graces of the sacrament of matrimony. Both were very frail and shared a room in the skilled nursing unit. Then Al died.

"Virginia's constant refrain to me and to her loving family was "I miss Al. I miss him so much." I often suggested that she send her love to Al and told her that Al would send his love back to her. And so over the months, Virginia sent her love to Al in her prayers. She continued to tell him over and over how much she loved him and missed him. One day she informed me, "I have been sending my love to Al but he does not answer back." Virginia died after longing for her Al for a year and a half. The day before she left us, I assured her "You and Al will be dancing joyfully forever in eternal life." The smile she gave me will also last into eternal life where our loved ones are not far away."

—Fr. Richard F. Berg, C.S.C., in *Fragments of Hope*, 4-6.

"Without hope—or in despair—the spiritual life withers. One may feel, 'my confidence seems so shattered, my vision obscure. Why take the time or make the effort to move ahead?' These are the moments when we need to pray for hope or have someone praying for us. It is during these silent or prayerful moments that promises may be remembered.

"The promise of hope sparks the soul. Hope prompts us to begin again or set out with new confidence. Hope pulls us through the challenges and dark times. Hope reminds us of those very familiar images of making our way toward the light at the end of the tunnel or of the moth drawn to the light of the candle. Hope is about motion, moving us on with some new assurance.

"A mere glimmer of hope from the divine brightness of God radiates in our human soul. As we move closer to the inner light, intimacy with our creator deepens to the point that God-light may be so bright that we feel blinded and overwhelmed in the face of God. Some saints who were drawn very close to God speak of their experience of brightness as a new kind of darkness, devoid of human consolations and spiritual pleasures. But with hopeful trust, they continued to move ahead welcoming and embracing the Kingdom of God in their lives and world.

"The motto of my religious organization, Holy Cross, is 'The cross is our only hope.'

"By this we understand that, like Christ, we are called

to move through life shouldering burdens and sufferings with others. The daily cross of giving our lives for others is to be understood as a gift. It is a lifelong process of serving others while dying to self that leads to the promise of resurrection. It is also a daily event of hopefulness....

"The cross of Christ is everywhere in the world; and so is the hope it brings."

—Fr. Richard Berg, C.S.C., in *Fragments of Hope*, 129-130

"WHEN TIMES become darker, let your light shine more brightly. You will encounter rough times and some people who do not wish you well. It will be easy to become demoralized and want to quit. As Winston Churchill said, 'If you're going through hell, keep going...' So be wise about whom you allow access to your inner spirit. When something doesn't feel right, listen to that, take action to protect yourself, find ways to keep your spirit up in the dark times.

"You have nothing to lose. Go for it. Spending time dwelling on your faults and fears is a waste of time. Yes, do learn from them, but don't let them stop you from doing what you are called to do. Your mistakes and setbacks can teach you the most important information to make you succeed in your journey. Reaching for your goals may actually lead to better things of which you were not even aware. God's working in your life is real. You will be amazed how God guided you and accompanied you through your life journey even when you thought you had failed. It will all make sense eventually. Embrace the story that is your life."

—Dominic Vachon, "Gve Your Life Back to the World," in *A Letter to My Freshman Self*, 2, 13-14.

Struggles of Notre Dame

"*If* PHYSICAL TRIALS and hardships had overcome the Fathers of Notre Dame, the little cabin on your campus would represent the limits of their missionary efforts in this great Midwest.

"*If* the struggle against poverty had broken the spirit of parents and grandparents, there would never have been the resources to send you here to obtain the benefits of Catholic culture.

"*If* seemingly overwhelming odds meant surrender, there never would have been the glorious tradition of athletic prowess, for indeed it is the will to win regardless of the odds that stirred this nation with the symbol of 'the fighting Irish.'

"*If* misfortune crushed Notre Dame, then the great fire of 1879 which wiped out every University building except the chapel and the theater would have written 'Finis' to Notre Dame. But in the two remaining buildings—the chapel and the stage of life upon which generations should perpetuate Catholic teaching—there was a symbolic meaning for the Fathers of Notre Dame

"*If* the Fathers of the Noble Congregation of Holy Cross had fastened their gaze upon earth alone and placed their prize upon the praise of men, there would never have been the grotto by the lake where stalwart generations of Notre Dame students have knelt reverently in deep devotion and prayer to God."

Those triumphs over adversities spell for you the lesson of after-life."

—Joseph P. Kennedy, in *Go Forth and Do Good*, 132-33.

NOTRE DAME IS....

Home. A place where young spirits and hope soar, and hope flames brightly on faces and in hearts, where consolation and healing await the weary, a place where sorrow and self doubt, failure and loss can be brought to the railing at the Grotto and entrusted to the Lady who stands watch over all who come there.

"*A Holy Site* to people who never lived here or studied here, but in some real and mysterious way, let it have a place in their life. For some, it is a sign, a goal, a tabernacle, a favorite place (even though unvisited), a destination. For Catholics, it stands as proof of a coming of age in America, against the odds, in the face of intolerance, with no diminishing of faith.

"*A Font of Grace.* Almost as if it is a field of favor, this place takes hold, sometimes even of the most recalcitrant, and removes the scales from eyes so they can see again- or maybe for the first time- with the vision of faith. Miracles happen here – little ones and big ones —insights, decisions, acceptance, rejuvenation, teased out by some power that reaches the mind and soul. Hardness of heart finds no easy home here; magnanimity, bigness of soul, is in the land and landscape. The graves of the unsung heroes who built the place, brick by brick, who cleaned and baked, cooked and cared, are nearby and somehow the spirit of giving all for the common good is in the air breathed here, a legacy that emanates from those who were here before us and that, with our touches added, will be here for those who come after us, for all time.

"*Classrooms* with a crucifix on the wall, a silent reminder that knowledge and truth need to culminate in goodness. Preparation for life, not simply for a profession happens here; there is no such thing as Catholic chemistry, but there is such a thing as a worldview that sees all of nature through eyes of faith and so catches nuances and tones that do not distort the picture; they simply make it whole.

"*Notre Dame* is Father Hesburgh making the University home for European intellectuals fleeing communism, or welcoming Monsignor Jack Egan, the great social justice activist, when his work was curtailed by the Archbishop of Chicago. Once, when I published at Notre Dame Press a book critical of Cardinal Cody and it brought episcopal wrath to Fr. Ted's door, I offered to resign. Fr. Ted sent me a note saying simply, "We don't punish people at Notre Dame for responsible use of free speech."

"*People*, generation after generations of them, here to study, write, teach, pray, work; privileged to be in the company of other searchers in a place dedicated to Mary, the Mother of Jesus. It is a family and it can trace its immediate lineage back to 1842, and its real ancestry back more than two millennia. Like every family, it has its share of dysfunction. Unlike every family it also has the resources and the will to act in the best interest of the individual and the community as a whole. It is possible that there is no place on earth with a greater concentration of good people. No one who comes here seeking solace, inspiration, knowledge or care leaves unchanged. Like it or not, sense it or not, to come here is to be touched by and to take away some portion of the grace that seems to spring from the very ground. Not to worry; the supply is infinite.

"*Memories* shared by alumni, staff, and faculty, active and emeriti, of friends and friendships, of dorm life and homesickness, of dances and pep rallys, of the lakes and the lights on the dome, of Masses that uplifted, teachers who inspired, of talks long and deep that probed the very mystery of life. Physical presence here might now seem only a snapshot in time, like the photos of the south quad filled with the formation of men in uniform training for battle during World War II, or earlier, the pictures of young men standing on campus next to unicycles brought back from Europe by Father Sorin. The spots where they stood are still there, still identifiable. You can still stand where Knute Rockne did when he was baptized in the Log Chapel on November 20, 1925. Or where his casket rested in Sacred Heart Church.

"Some day people will look at images of those on campus now and pause for a moment to marvel not at the changes, but at the continuity. No one who has ever walked near the Dome at night will forget how little and how large it made them feel just to be there. The statue of Father Sorin faces toward Notre Dame Avenue so that he can welcome his sons and daughters home. Again."

—Jim Langford, in *The Times of My Life*, 215-218.

Dreams

"Dreams don't die
Sometimes they hibernate
Deep in that cavernous place inside you
In the broken places
In the weary places
In the exhausted places
Right next to the place that feels it can't go on
But you must
Dreams don't die
They rest nestled abutted right next to the soul
Dreams don't die
And they don't care
About how shattered you are
About how broken you are
About how tired you are
They just dare you
Because they believe they are stallions
Desirous of freedom
Waiting for their chance to run unhinged
By the past or anxieties of the future
And you should
Let them."

—by Fee Thomas

"THE GOSPEL and the teaching of Jesus reminds us constantly that we are always most properly judged in terms of our interior life rather than our public persona. In the end, the Christian paradox is that we are taught in the Gospel about the great reversal at the end of time, that those who are first in the world's eyes will be among the last and the last will be among the first. Those who are considered great in the Kingdom of God are those who have been the servants of the rest. At the end of one's life, it is not the fame that one has achieved or the economic success or political power, but rather the legacy of dedicated service that one leaves behind. Worldly success does not last forever and it is our responsibility to seek to make a positive difference in the world, especially in light of those who carry the heaviest burden during their earthly existence. The Christian paradox is ultimately a very positive message, for it gives all of us hope that, whatever our condition in life, we are beloved by God and that no set of temporary disadvantages can ever estrange us from the love and mercy of God."

—Fr. Monk Malloy, C.S.C., in *Monk's Musings*, 24.

"FULLY A THIRD of the gospels tell of Jesus healing the body and mind. In particular, He gives sight to the blind. He raises the dead. He honors the body and intends to show that God gave human beings life and wishes that life to flourish. There is to be 'the resurrection of the body and life everlasting.' God is a God of the living. He does not preside over a cemetery of ages past. We shall see each other again.

"When a child is born, a treasure of great price has been given us, for only human beings live forever. Monuments of granite will become dust from the erosion of wind and rain, given enough time. Only human beings have the hope of everlasting life, and life in the company of the God of life itself, the God who does not have life but is life. We shall share God's life and live forever in God's presence.

"We know we are born to die. We are mortal and our bodies will age beyond repair. Death need not be a dead end, however. Death can be a beginning of a new life. The child is born from its mother's womb into this vast and glorious world far surpassing life in the womb. Similarly, persons who believe in eternal life with God believe that they are born again from out of the womb of this body that is the world. When we die we are going to the wedding with the God we have loved within and behind all the other loves of our life in this world. We do not go to our funeral, we go to our wedding; our friends and family attend us at our funeral....

"A world that God has begun and will finish contains and celebrates 'in the ending' every good and true meaning that has ever entered the heart and mind of humankind. We live in such hope. 'Eye has not seen, nor ear heard, neither have entered into the heart of man, the things which God has prepared for them that love him.' I Cor 2:9."

—Fr. Nicholas Ayo C.S.C.,
in *Your God May Be Too Small*, 74,75,92-3

"EVERY COMMUNITY needs stories to sustain its common life. We talk about heroic figures from the past and examples of individuals whose deeds and style of life continue to inspire us. In the Christian life, we tell stories of great men and women whom we call saints because in one way or another they personified the Gospel. Thus, Mary the mother of Jesus, St. Paul the Apostle to the Gentiles, Francis of Assisi, Teresa of Avila, and more contemporary figures like Francis Xavier Cabrini, Andre Bessette, and Pope John XXIII are exemplars of the Gospel.

"In a sense, saints are religious all-stars. They provide the power of example; they are the personification of giftedness in the power of the Holy Spirit.

"In contrast, public sinners know the agony of defeat. They have, for whatever reason, failed to live by the values that they proclaim. As a result, either civil society or the Church community holds them accountable for their misdeeds. This does not mean that public sinners are abandoned but rather they stand in stark contrast to the saints among us. Reprobates are those who try to change the rules to serve themselves. They often appear prosperous in the public eye, but have gained their preeminence by unsavory means. This is true not only of individuals who rob banks or engage in narcotics trafficking, or kill people for money, but also those in the upper echelons who have taken advantage of the inability of individuals and groups to protect themselves from harm."

—Fr. Monk Malloy, C.S.C., in *Monk's Musings*, 24.

"WE BEGAN THIS BOOK by referring to the woman at the well. Have you ever noticed what she did after her encounter with Jesus? The gospel says she left her bucket behind her when she left. Having found the one who eliminates further thirst, she didn't need her water jar anymore. Through Jesus, she was touched by the God who unconditionally loved; she received 'living water,' a fountain within, leaping up to provide eternal life.

"Just as we stood with that woman at the beginning, with our own thirst and our buckets in hand, we are meant to stand with her now—and share that living water. And dare to believe that because of the risen life we experience, death and hatred and despair will not have the last word. No, the last word is not 'exit' but 'entrance'; not 'dearly departed' but 'newly arrived'; not 'Sorry about that' but Welcome home!"

—Fr. Bill Toohey, C.S.C., in *Fully Alive*, 115-116.

"THE SAINTS are sinners who kept trying."

—Robert Louis Stevenson

"IT IS GOD'S REPUTATION that He tracks down people because in some mysterious way, God needs each of us and all of us. Sinful and fickle as we are, we are His family, and God will leave the ninety-nine good sheep to search for the lost one. Most of us don't hear God calling us by name. But God knows where we are better than we do and accommodates our manner of knowing by sending both signs and the software necessary to read them."

—Jim Langford, in *Walking with God in a Fragile World*, 26-7.

"WHILE PASSING THROUGH Grand Central Station in New York City, I noticed a woman sitting beside a wall near one of the trains. Like an empty, lifeless shell, she sat slumped with her head over her knees. After buying an extra cup of coffee, I sat down with her and asked 'How are things going?'

Guardedly, she said, 'Fine.'

'How has the day been?'

'Good,' she said defensively.

'What's new?

'Nothing,' she said. Then she turned away and shut me down, as if a wall had come between us.

"We sat together in silence for nearly twenty minutes and then she turned my way and said, 'Who the hell are you, anyways?'

"I answered, I'm a priest, and I just thought you needed

a cup of coffee." Unexpectedly, she started to cry intensely. After a long period of silence, I asked, 'What is your name?'

She said, 'Sara.' She then began to describe her cross— her life, its struggles and broken relationships. Seeing Christ Jesus in her worn and weary face, I asked, 'Sara if you could change anything in the world today, what would it be?'

"There was a long pause, but then she said, 'I would change my mind Only then might I find a way out of the prison of my own heart.' As we sat together and drank our coffee, I experienced a glimmer of the hope born of the Cross of Christ. It was as if I could hear Jesus' words, 'You are not far from the Kingdom of God.'"

—Daniel G. Groody,C.S.C. in *The Cross Our Only Hope*, (Dec.5)

"THE CROSS MEANS many things to many people. To some, the cross gives value to suffering as redemptive. To others it gives warrant to seek suffering, as if suffering was not what Jesus all his life tried to relieve. A third of the Gospel tells of Jesus healing every kind of physical, mental and emotional suffering. I think the cross is about the beauty and wonder of existence. To be called into a material world, to take a journey with God as my companion, to exist merely and wondrously in the miracle of sharing God's very existence, that is the meaning of the cross. Our existence, taken from nothingness, cannot be in the world without suffering, however small or great, infrequent or frequent. To live is to suffer, and to live, to be, to exist in even dire circumstance has a value beyond nothingness that can never be compared to anything at all. If there is a God, the creation will be fulfilled in God's eternal life, for God and goodness is convertible. The world will have a happy ending. In the meantime, creation and redemption suffer a time of the cross, which is why we can never lose sight of the cross. We live in a world where there is no escaping the passages and ravages of time and human decision. The choice we do have is to carry our cross hopefully or to drag it reluctantly. When we fall under its weight, we can only hope in God to lift us to do what can be done to relieve human suffering. Jesus did not explain the cross. Jesus carried his cross in solidarity with us and his promise is that someday we will see that human existence was a blessing beyond all suffering, because the God of such mystery went before us."

" 'Thy will be done' is never a prayer of resignation, but one always with its moment of grace and truth."

—Nicholas Ayo, C.S.C., in *The Heart of Notre Dame*, 110-111, 143.

"AN IMPORTANT PRINCIPLE of prayer is this: one prays as one can, not as one ought. Loosen your grip on the shoulds and should-nots of prayer. It's a grip that will stifle the awareness of God's presence in your life. You and the Father and Spirit and Jesus are involved in a dance of life that changes from day to day, even minute to minute. To say that 'I ought' to pray this way and no other is to tell God that I am only this one particular dance step and no other. God will dance with you because He loves you and wants to be with you. But his dancing will be wistful and sad, because he can only do what you will allow him to do, and he'd much rather sweep you off your feet and into the universe of his love."

—Fr. Herb Yost, C.S.C. *Waiting in Joyful Hope*,129.

"SPIRIT is hard to define. It is a fire in the belly, a sense of purpose, a reason for getting up in the morning and doing our best all day, every day. May our spirit grow in defense of those we love, those we need, and those who need us.

"I HOPE WE CAN rebuild our country into a home where hardness of heart finds no easy entrance; where magnanimity—bigness of soul—is encouraged and embraced... where the spirit of giving all for the common good is in the air we breathe as a legacy from those who were here before us and that, with our touches added, will be here for all who come after us, for all time."

—Jim Langford

"THAT IS LOVE, to give away everything, to sacriface everything, without the slighest desire to get anything in return."

—Albert Camus

"ABSOLUTELY PROFOUND words to stir the heart: "There must come a time in everyone's life when he or she is uplifted to the stars because of something good he or she does with whole heart and soul. It does not matter whether this lasts for years or hours or seconds. What matters is that it happens at all. One who lives a hundred years, who has not been lifted up, even a second, dies stillborn."

—Martin Schneider.

WILLIAM JAMES WROTE, "the greatest use in life is spending yourself in something that will outlast you."

LOVE

"In the long run, what really matters is who and what you loved, the example you set for others, the way you accepted the good and not good in your life. And, above all, the grace that God sent through you to those who needed your embrace, your words, your inspiration...and your love."

—Jim Langford

Doing Mercy:
Another Week at the Border

EACH DAY ICE brings 8 to 10 refugees to Sister Nor-ma's Humanitarian Respite Center. On Tuesday I met a woman from Honduras. She was pregnant. We talked for a little bit and I asked her how things went when she crossed the border. She said that things went well. I asked her, "Did they let you cross because you're pregnant?" She said, "No, I crossed because of the grace and good-ness of God." She didn't know that I am a priest. So she did not say this to impress me. Rather the words just flowed from her heart. The poor can teach us so much about true dependence on God, not just saying it, but knowing it from the inside out.

I also met a family of four from Honduras --- dad and mom and two sons. The six year old was born with an illness. He is always in a lying down position. He has never been able to sit up or stand up. He is fed with a stomach pump of some sort. He has no control of his bod-ily functions. He is completely dependent upon his parents for everything. He cannot speak. The five year old son is completely and totally a five year old boy.

I talked with them for almost an hour. I wanted to learn about them and from them. When the six year old son was born, the hospital told the parents that the boy would not live long and there was nothing that they could do for him. And they didn't do anything. The parents devoted themselves completely to their son. Now six years later they decide to try to come to the United States where they might be able to get medical care for their son. Their love for him is immense. And though he has never spoken a word, I loved watching the five year old communicate with his six year old brother.

Since the boy has never been able to stand up and is held and carried everywhere, I kept wondering how they were able to get to the US / Mexico border from Honduras. So I asked them. They pushed their son in a stroller from Honduras to the border. I can't even begin to imagine what that would have been like. I just can't. I was already crying as they told me the story, but when they got to the part of how they crossed the Rio Grande River with their son in a stroller on a raft of some sort, I just wept. As I write these words I try to imagine what it would have been like to put the stroller on a raft and accompany the boy across the river.

On Wednesday we spent a good portion of the day at the La Lomita chapel in Mission, Texas. No one knows for certain when La Lomita chapel was built, but

sometime around 1849. Though tiny in size— 12' by 25'
— the history of the chapel and the role that it has played
in the life of the Church in southern Texas is very big. La
Lomita Chapel is a point of pride is for the Oblates of
Mary Immaculate (OMI). It would be virtually impossible
to understand how the Church developed and flourished
in southern Texas from Brownsville to Roma without understanding the OMIs and this chapel. The chapel served
as headquarters for the Oblates serving five other chapels,
75 ranches and numerous villages throughout Hidalgo
county. In years past the Oblates slept in the chapel going
from one mission to the next. It is only fitting that on many
occasions Fr. Roy Snipes, OMI, the Pastor of Our Lady
of Guadalupe Parish in Mission, Texas, and of La Lomita
chapel has found refugees sleeping in the chapel at night,
just having crossed the River and looking for a place to
spend the night before heading out the next day.

The chapel has become somewhat "famous" in the
past ten years. Why? The chapel is very close to the Rio
Grande River. If the wall is ever built between the United
States and Mexico, the chapel would be on the south side
of the wall, which means that no one could get to it. It
would be in the United States but on the south side of
the wall. It would be between the wall and the river. So it

would be in a "no man's land" so to speak. So how could a person go there to pray or go there for Mass? People go there day and night to pray. Mass is celebrated every Friday morning. They would have to get on to the other side of the wall…and they would not be able to do so. Both the Bishop of Brownsville and the Provincial Superior of the Oblates of Mary Immaculate have spoken very strongly about this. Even if the wall is built, there will have to be a way for people to get to this chapel. Just one more reason why the wall is a terrible idea. Father Roy has a big magnet on his car door with the image of Our Lady of Guadalupe. It reads "No Walls Between Amigos."

Fr. Roy took us for a boat ride on the Rio Grande River. There were Border Control towers everywhere and Border Control boats going back and forth. I understand that they are doing their job. The width of the river was, at most, 20 - 25 yards. When you are that close to a border, it all seems so arbitrary and even unnecessary. I took an empty water bottle and filled it with water from the Rio Grande River—holy water, made holy by God who created it and by the thousands of families who have crossed the river in search of a better life for them and their children. I was almost afraid to put the bottle in the water fearing that the alligators and crocodiles threatened by the current administration would be there.

On Thursday along with the Notre Dame students here for a border immersion program, I visited one of the detention centers run by Customs and Border Protection. We were welcomed by several officers who were very kind and gracious to us. We were given a brief orientation and then had to turn over our cell phones and put them in lockers. We were told that if anyone was caught using a cell phone while we went through the center that he/she would be escorted out immediately. There was almost a paranoia about anything being filmed or recorded.

I thought that I was ready for what I would see. But I was not. When we went into the interior of the building we could see hundreds of people—men, women, and children—locked up in cages, a total of 427 people. Many were sleeping on the floor covered with these space-looking blankets. We were told that this is the approximate number that is arrested each day and brought to this detention center. I will never be able to get this sight out of my mind —hundreds of people in locked cages. I wore my Roman collar and many people called out to me, "Padre, Padre." I cannot put into words the helplessness that I felt as people called out to me saying "Padre" and I could do nothing except greet them in return.

The officers were polite and kind. They talk about

their job. Like everyone else they tell of their work from their perspective, which is never the entire story. They would have you believe that every person that they apprehend is a criminal. And we have to be protected from these criminals. This is not the case at all. The overwhelming majority are people searching for a better life for their family and children. That is why they flee their country in search of asylum. Think—a family running out of a burning house. People never leave their house willingly, but if it's burning, then they have to leave.

Another example of telling the story from one's perspective is this. The law that will not allow people to cross the border from Mexico into the United States is known as "Migrant Protection Protocols." Protection? Anything but protection. The spin on the name is revelatory. The more accurate name is "Remain in Mexico."

Towards the end of the presentation, I said to the presenter, "Why do you do this job?" The man who answered the question seemed uncomfortable with the question and sort of dodged the question. It's a job and he needs a paycheck to feed and clothe and house his family. I am sure that he is a good man, a good husband, and a good father. One thought that I had as we left the detention center is this; at what point does a person decide that they cannot do a particular job? At what point is their faith and their job irreconcilable?

At the end of the presentation I said to the officer, "I want so much to dislike you, but I can't." Then I thanked him for putting a human face to Customs and Border Protection.

On Friday I went to the Respite Center. I helped make lunch and gave out clothing to families who would be traveling to another city today. There was a woman there with a baby. I learned that her other child was in the hospital having had surgery last week. Her husband was with this child. I asked her if she wanted a ride to the hospital to see her daughter. She jumped at the idea and off we went --- she, her baby, and me. She sat in the back seat with her baby who was in a car seat.

At one point she shrieked. As usual I thought that it was my bad driving. I asked her what was wrong. She said, "Se me olvido mi grillete." I learned a new word in Spanish—"grillete." That's the word for those ankle bracelets the ICE puts on you when you are in the US without documents, but with permission. She said that she forgot to put the battery in her ankle bracelet when we left the Center. She had been charging it. So we called the Center and asked someone to bring it to her in the hospital.

The whole thing made me so sad. This poor woman with an ankle bracelet that tracks her every step so that ICE knows where she is at all times.

The will to begin fixing this broken system is not there. That's the problem. Shame on us. We are talking about families and children who are suffering greatly. So many children suffering so much. May God have mercy on us for our indifference.

Lord Jesus Christ, Son of the Living God, have mercy on me a sinner.

—Fr. Joseph Corpora, C.S.C., in
Doing Mercy, to be published by Corby Books in 2020.

From the Monks at Weston Priory, Vt

"I want to say something to all of you
Who have become a part of the fabric of my life.
The color and texture
Which you have brought into
My being
Have become a song,
And I want to sing
It forever.
There is an energy in us

Which makes things happen
When the paths of other persons
Touch ours
And we have to be there
And let it happen.
When the time
Of our particular sunset comes
Our thing, our accomplishment
Won't really matter
A great deal.
But the clarity and care
With which we have loved others
Will speak with vitality
Of the great gift of life
We have been for each other."

"That is love, to give away everything, to sacrifice everything, without the slightest desire to get anything in return."

—Albert Camus

"LOVE MEANS A LOT TO ME, because I see so much of it in my work in campus ministry. I see much of it every day; and some days are specially filled with love's dimensions. For example, during last school year I went to Dayton, Ohio, to attend the funeral of one of our students, who was killed in a tragic automobile accident. I saw many manifestations of love on that occasion. I found out what love means. Love means —well, it means a mother and father who are torn with pain over the death of their oldest son, and yet can think of only being gracious and kind and sensitive to the needs of others, wonderfully hospitable to the relatives and friends who were with them on that occasion. Love means—well, love means the grandmother of this student, herself dying of cancer, yet the most outgoing, energetic, least self-pitying person in the crowd. Love means three carloads of Notre Dame students, who got up at four-thirty on a winter morning and drove through a northern Indiana blizzard to participate in the funeral Mass and burial of their friend.

"The song is right: 'What the world needs now is love, sweet love; that's the only thing that there's too little of.' But it seems there's more to it than that. Although there is indeed a great lack of love, such a tremendous need for more love in this world, there are also—if we look at the total picture, fantastic demonstrations and manifestations of love around us all the time. We ought to see this.

We ought to rejoice in it, thank God for it....recognize him in it. For, after all, love is his name."

— William Toohey, C.S.C., in *A Passion for the Possible*, 83.

"DOES LOVE stand a chance? We are surrounded with so many causes for pessimism that one really begins to wonder. Pessimism follows from statistics, from the brutal facts of life that we see around us.

"But there is another side to the picture. I am becoming more and more convinced that it is not only possible but indeed absolutely necessary for us to be simultaneously pessimistic and hopeful. One does not cancel out the other. Statistics lead us to pessimism, but man does not live by statistics alone. There is more than the tangible, measurable facts we see around us. There is a spirit alive in this land. There is a spirit alive, and love has a chance because the God who is love, now risen and glorious, remains in our midst. As he tried to tell us over and over again, he is 'Emmanuel'--God with us. He promised that he would remain with us to the end of time. So love is here because he is here, trying to continue his own ministry of concern and compassion through us, in our loveless world.

"Consequently, in the midst of the pessimism we are led to by the statistics mounting all around us, we are also led to hope; not only permitted to hope, but impelled to hope, to have a passion for the possible. As a contemporary banner declares, 'Don't leave town—there's still hope.'"

"So this is no time for despair or increased cynicism.

If anything, we need to renew idealism, to declare that love does stand a chance, to develop a passion for the possible. Does love stand a chance?

If it doesn't, neither do we."

—William Toohey C.S.C., *A Passion for the Possible*, 90-92.

"'IF WE HUNGER AND THIRST for righteousness' we are called to become active in the world. Institutions such as the government or the Church cannot fight for what is right by themselves: they need hard-working, dedicated people to make a real difference. "Making a difference requires an understanding of the sacredness of life. Before we can venture beyond our own walls and into the lives of others, we must realize just how special we are. We must love ourselves. We must acknowledge that there is a higher purpose to our lives than simply 'making it' from day to day. Once we recognize the sacredness in ourselves, we can turn our attention to those around us There is a danger, however, to loving ourselves too much. In a world that overemphasizes the self—self help, individual progress, financial prowess—we sometimes forget the world around us. We become consumed with our own lives Some call it survival. Society teaches us to look out for number one. But it doesn't teach us that if we spend all our time looking out solely for ourselves, we someday encounter a painful loneliness. Happiness depends on our relationship to the world, to others.

"By being charitable—giving of ourselves for the sake of others—we find positive ways to use our time. We might serve food at a homeless shelter, donate money to a needy family, or volunteer to teach literacy classes. There are many virtues, many ingredients for living a moral, happy life, but charity is the one that 'binds everything together in perfect harmony (Colossians 3:14) Charity upholds and purifies our human ability to love. It calls us to give something of ourselves, to love others so much that we go out of our way to help them find happiness and enjoy life."

—Jim Langford, in *Happy Are They*, 29-30.

"If love is the soul of Christian existence, it must be at the heart of every other Christian virtue. Thus, for example, justice without love is legalism; faith without love is ideology; hope without love is self-centeredness; forgiveness without love is self-abasement; fortitude without love is recklessness; generosity without love is extravagance; care without is mere duty; fidelity without love is mere servitude. Every virtue is an expression of love."

—Fr. Richard McBrien, in *Catholicism*, 977.

(*When I first came upon the poetry of Fee Thomas, a young, black writer from Minnesota, I became an immediate fan. Her poetry hits hard in an immediate kind of way. She says things directly, but with a style that is her own. I selected a few poems from the volume Corby Books will soon publish.*)

Dedicated to Saint Mary Magdalene

" AND I LOVE HER. In a way I don't completely understand. In a way that defies comprehension. In a way too thick for mere language. And I love her. In a way that is out of my self. In a space that is sacred. In a place wrapped in yellow. In somewhere that is not destination. And I love her. With tears that know no shame. Limbs that know no weight. A Spirit reaching inward. And I love her. In the deep mist where she leads me. Her hair fragrant. The angels praising her. Jesus's eyes on her head. And I love her. While she holds out her hands. Draws me close. Whispers my name. Tells me it's okay."

—Fee Thomas

"SOME YEARS AGO, Jim and Jill Langford started a day camp for inner-city kids, ages 4-12 on 15 acres in the country, just south of South Bend. With the help of many donors, they built trails through nine acres of woods, a baseball field, basketball court volleyball court, a clubhouse with a large fireplace and an auditorium for blossoming performing artists.

"One day Jim brought in a van full of kids. When he pulled up to the camp, the children were so eager to hit the ground running that they barely waited for the van to stop. That is, all the children but one little girl.

"As the kids raced from the van with all the energy kids have, this little girl moped her way across the field. Jill had been observing the little girl and silently decided to dedicate herself to getting a smile from her. As it turned out, the child came from an abusive home, and, though she undoubtedly enjoyed moments of freedom the camp provided, she dreaded the end of the day when she would again be subjected to the trauma of abuse.

"As the kids got a hot game of kickball going, the little girl seemed less than interested. But she took her turn at the plate, kicked the ball and made it to first. As she stopped on the base she noticed that Jill was clapping and cheering. She looked around as if to say, 'You couldn't possibly be cheering for me. Nobody cheers for me.' But it suddenly dawned on her that Jill was, indeed, cheering her on.

"Jill's cheering and subtle gestures of love lasted through the day. And bit by bit the little girl seemed to perk up until she eventually smiled.

"At the end of the day, in a moment Jill says she will never forget, the little girl said something that the greatest theologians and mystics have struggled to say for centuries. As the children got into the van, the little girl ran over to Jill and asked her to take off the sunglasses she had been wearing throughout that bright, sunny day.

'Why', Jill asked.

'Because," the girl said, 'I want to see your eyes so that I can know you and remember you.'

"Jill took off her sunglasses and the tears welled up in her eyes as she and this little girl met eye to eye, soul to soul. After a hug, the little girl ran to board the van. A fleeting moment of unsolicited love became a God moment that will last for a lifetime for a little girl, a grown woman, and all who hear the story.

"For who among us does not to peer into another's eyes and know the bond of love. Who among us does not want to be surprised by someone's care or surprise another with our care? And who among us does not want one day to enjoy the beatific vision of staring directly into God's eyes only to discover that we have been staring into them all along?" —Jeremy Langford, in *God Moments*, 184-85.

Scars of Love

"SOME YEARS AGO on a hot summer day in south Florida a little boy decided to go for a swim in the old swimming hole behind his house. He flew into the water, not realizing that as he swam toward the middle of the lake, an alligator was swimming toward the shore. His mother was in the house, looking out the window and saw the two as they got closer and closer. In utter fear, she ran toward the water, yelling to her son as loudly as she could. Hearing her voice, the little boy became alarmed and made a U turn to swim to his mother. It was too late. Just as he reached her, the alligator reached him. From the dock, the mother grabbed her little boy by the arms just as the alligator snatched his legs. That began an incredible tug-of-war between the two. The alligator was much stronger than the mother, but the mother was much too passionate to let go. A farmer happened to drive by, heard her screams, raced from his truck and shot the alligator.

"Remarkably, after weeks in the hospital, the little boy survived. His legs were extremely scarred by the vicious attach of the animal. And, on his arms, were deep scratches where his mother's fingernails dug into his flesh in her effort to hang on to the son she loved. The newspaper reporter who interviewed the boy after the trauma, asked if he would show him his scars. The boy lifted his pant legs. And then, with obvious pride, he said to the reporter, 'I have great scars on my arms too. I have them because my Mom wouldn't let go.'

"We can identify with that little boy. We have scars too, the scars from a painful past. Some of those scars are unsightly and have caused us deep regret. But some wounds are because God has refused to let go. He promises, 'I give them eternal life, and they shall never perish, and no one shall snatch them out of my hand. My Father, who has given them to me, is greater than all, and no one is able to snatch them out of the Father's hand.' In the midst of your struggle, He's been there holding on to you. This day take hope that our Lord is totally committed to your highest good and to the highest good of those you love."

—Kathy Sullivan, in *I Had Lunch With God*, 58.

IN ADDITION TO BEING University Chaplin and Rector of Keenan Hall at Notre Dame, Father Griffin, known as Griff, assisted in St. Joseph's Church in New York's Greenwich Village during vacation periods and spent countless late-night hours befriending, counseling and accompanying the alcoholics, drug addicts, runaways, prostitutes and panhandlers of Times Square....He remembers one might say, the forgotten people When I forget or am forgotten myself, I hope a Robert Griffin is there...

"The media titan Ted Turner once famously denounced Christianity as 'a religion for losers.' Griff was exactly what Turner had in mind when he spoke of losers. If to be a loser is to be an obese, lonely, insecure, nicotine-addicted and fretful priest, who is temporarily employed by a success-fixated institution and perpetually tormented with a gnawing sense that he is living a fatally-diminished life, Griff was a loser.

"Griff was a loser as Father Damien of Molokai was a leper. He was a priest for the losers and lost of the campus of Notre Dame and the streets of Manhatten. He knew in his flesh and spirit the agonies of the awkward adolescent, the drug-addled student, the battered whore, the homesick runaway, the embarrassed misfit, the disconsolate solitary and the utter loon. For each of these, he had a warm and ready welcome; in each of these, he sought and served the Loser's Christ; to each of these, he showed the face of the Lord who had found him.

"We must beg God to send us more losers like him."

—Michael Garvey, Intro to *The Kingdom of the Lonely God*,16-20

"HE [FATHER GRIFFIN] did look clownish,I guess: surely the most awkward man on campus. Large and heavy, baby-faced even when unshaved, unkempt hair escaping from a shabby cap, elephant trousers flecked with cigarette ash, a cocker spaniel named Darby O'Gill yanking its leash between the ankles, Griff would shamble across the North Quad. Griff was University chaplain for 30 years...A missionary to the lonely, nobody has ever loved us so much. Griff once wrote,'You cannot sing a night song until the hour before dawn, when the darkness has nearly ended. Then, when loneliness has worn you out, you understand, in an insight as spontaneous as laughter, that God has been keeping watch'...His was the simple but ineluctably vital ministry of being there"

—Luis Gamez, Notre Dame, 1997.

RESPONDING to an anonymous letter from a student expressing deep pain in his life, Griff wrote:

"Everywhere I look, within myself or outside myself, I find that the ground is covered by birds with broken wings. Rarely among the children of this world does one find a human being who is as fully endowed or unblemished as he feels he must be to take to the air and sail the sky and lift himself into the pathway of the sun where the trail of the rainbow begins.

But a bird must learn to trust his wings, broken or otherwise...

"In other words, young sir, know your own beauty and use it, if you feel imperfect in some detail, remember that other men are also imperfect. In this flawed, faulty world, the girl with a perfect body is born with a cleft lip, the boy with the soul of an athlete is handicapped with a cripple's foot, a scholar who loves his mind discovers that madness runs in his family line, the saint with a passion for God is daily teased by the demons of apostasy.

"I once heard of a man who sold a flock of homing pigeons to an ornithologist who lived in a town 25 miles away. To ground the pigeons in their new hutch, the ornithologist clipped the wings of the birds so that they could not return to their original home. Two weeks later, the first owner looked out the window; there, trudging down the road, were the pigeons coming back to their natal roost. Unable to fly, the birds had walked over 25 miles on sore and bloody feet, to the spot that instinct told them was their own true home. Man's own true home is in the heart of God, and the pathway to the nesting place is through the lives of others, Whether on wings, or on tired and bloody feet, we must travel the road of love. Interestingly enough, we do not make the journey alone, but with others as maimed and clipped as ourselves.

Young stranger, I really can't think what to tell you about the choices you must make in the circumstances of a life that leaves you so lonely, but I am sure that somewhere there are special kinds of friends who are prepared to love you and be concerned about your welfare. But for them to accept you, you must first accept yourself as a being of sensibility and goodness, wisdom and grace. If at times your wing seems to be a bit more broken than all the others, remember that the falling sparrow was infinitely loveable to the One whose image is the gentleness of a Lamb, senselessly slaughtered on a cross of wood."

"At its best, my faith reflects the qualities—doubt, fear, passion, intensity, trust, courage, hope, grief—that are pre-occupying the students, children, colleagues, and friends of the Notre Dame community. For as a Christian, I am here not only to witness to faith, but also to find it incarnate in heartbeats that dance to the rhythms of grace."

—Robert Griffin, C.S.C., in *The Kingdom of the Lonely God.* 76

"THE GOD lonely enough to permit suffering is neither cruel not indifferent. The rumor that He dotes upon us like a hen nesting its chicks is not, despite evidence to the contrary, just a tale of myth-makers. People needing to love one another is what you're left with when you can't find God or when you shrink from him because of the pain. Loving one another, and being loved, is what He commanded us to do; it is a condition qualifying us for the fellowship of saints caught into joy in the Everlasting Arms: 'A man who does not love the brother that he can see cannot love God whom he has never seen.'

"All love, without exception, is a fulfillment of God's command. All love—puppy love, parent's love, sexual love, celibate love, saint's love, sinner's love, married love, courting love—all of it, if it is love, is an exercise of holy precepts, and is from the lifestream of the Trinity. Love, to achieve maturity, constantly needs self discipline and restraint; lovers must always guard themselves against love's parody, chiefly notable for its self indulgence.

"As long as you live with your heart in a hermitage, in flight from passion, you will never find healing. Like every other soul, you've got to take the risk of loving. Within the context of that experience, learn the cost of discipleship in the company of Christ who taught us that love makes its journey with a cross on its back.

"There are no easy roads to one's personal destiny in *The Kingdom of the Lonely God*."

Ibid 89-90

DEATH

"The Mystery of love is always the mystery of the cross. Love requires sacrifice, sooner or later... We must say goodbye to everything and everyone we love, in due time and due place. There is no joy without the cross, no eternal life with God in infinite joy without the passage of dying."

—Fr. Nicholas Ayo, C.S.C.

He was Grieving Over the Death of His Best Friend, Until an Old Man Told Him THIS...

This man perfectly explains the grieving process.
From the depths of old internet comments comes another
incredible gem of a story. One user wrote the following
heartfelt plea online:

"MY FRIEND JUST DIED. I don't know what to do."

The rest of the post has been deleted, only the title remains. However, the helpful responses live on, and one of them was absolutely incredible. The reply by this self-titled "old guy" might just change the way you approach life and death.

"I'm old. What that means is that I've survived (so far) and a lot of people I've known and loved did not.

"I've lost friends, best friends, acquaintances, co-workers, grandparents, mom, relatives, teachers, mentors, students, neighbors, and a host of other folks. I have no children, and I can't imagine the pain it must be to lose a child. But here's my two cents...

"I wish I could say you get used to people dying. But I never did. I don't want to. It tears a hole through me whenever somebody I love dies, no matter the circumstances. But I don't want it to "not matter". I don't want it to be something that just passes. My scars are a testament to the love and the relationship that I had for and with that person. And if the scar is deep, so was the love. So be it.

"Scars are a testament to life. Scars are a testament that I can love deeply and live deeply and be cut, or even gouged, and that I can heal and continue to live and continue to love. And the scar tissue is stronger than the original flesh ever was. Scars are a testament to life. Scars are only ugly to people who can't see.

"As for grief, you'll find it comes in waves. When the ship is first wrecked, you're drowning, with wreckage all around you. Everything floating around you reminds you of the beauty and the magnificence of the ship that was, and is no more. And all you can do is float. You find some piece of the wreckage and you hang on for a while. Maybe it's some physical thing. Maybe it's a happy memory or a photograph. Maybe it's a person who is also floating. For a while, all you can do is float. Stay alive.

"In the beginning, the waves are 100 feet tall and crash over you without mercy. They come 10 seconds apart and don't even give you time to catch your breath. All you can do is hang on and float. After a while, maybe weeks, maybe months, you'll find the waves are still 100 feet tall, but they come further apart. When they come, they still crash all over you and wipe you out. But in between, you can breathe, you can function. You never know what's going to trigger the grief. It might be a song, a picture, a street intersection, the smell of a cup of coffee. It can be just about anything...and the wave comes Somewhere down the line, and it's different for everybody, you find that the waves are only 80 feet tall. Or 50 feet tall. And while they still come, they come further apart. You can see them coming. An anniversary, a birthday, or Christmas, or landing at O'Hare. You can see it coming, for the most part, and prepare yourself. And when it washes over you, you know that somehow you will, again, come out the other side. Soaking wet, sputtering, still hanging on to some tiny piece of the wreckage, but you'll come out.

"Take it from an old guy. The waves never stop coming, and somehow you don't really want them to. But you learn that you'll survive them. And other waves will come. And you'll survive them too.

"If you're lucky, you'll have lots of scars from lots of loves. And lots of shipwrecks."

WHEN I WAS YOUNGER, I was braver. I was not afraid to die. My faith was strong and my health even stronger.

Vibrant vitality gives courage as nothing else. Now I am older. Now I am old. Now I feel weak around the knees and not so strong at heart. My faith may be in its twilight, not the dark night of the soul the saints endured, but a dusk not nearly so comfortable as yesteryear. I say it to myself for the first time. I am afraid to die. Of course I would have admitted that sooner, in a gesture of humility, but at the core I did not believe I was afraid to die. Now I say it. I am afraid to die, really afraid to die. Moreover, I am afraid of being afraid to die, and I am afraid of being afraid to die. Suddenly there is an infinite regress and the ground of my self- confidence seems like a challenge to walk on water. I think of a Woody Allen quip: 'I'm not afraid to die; I just don't want to be there when it happens.'

"My prayer life has become my night life, and my night life, spent recovering from the day's demands in a comfortable but lonely bed, has become my prayer life. If I am awake in bed, as often I am, it is dark and death is not un-thought of. Is not sleep a rehearsal for that opening night? I am afraid I will not know my lines, and even if I did, I might forget them. I am afraid to die and I admit how easy it has become to pray. There is no other resource left to me to cling to. Of course I can still parse my theology, but I expect to forget that too, and perhaps sooner than I think. Memory is not resource with a guarantee. And so I pray. I pray I will not forget how to pray. I continue to be afraid of being afraid, just as worrying about losing sleep loses sleep. perhaps I am just too anxious. "Who is afraid of Virginia Wolf"? Well, I am. And "Do not go gentle to that dark night"may be good advice, but I wonder if a protest or a fight would do any good. I may have lost my memory, and no doubt my courage, but I have not lost my mind – yet. And so I pray. And I prefer Jesus to the poets. "My God, my God, why have you forsaken me needs always to be balanced with what I hope never to forget: "Father, into thy hands I commend my spirit."

—Fr. Nicholas Ayo,C.S.C., in *The Heart of Notre Dame*, 266-67.

"GRIEF goes with our days and perhaps is a holy link with such horrors in the world as might find us otherwise hard of heart. Christ comforts us all."

—Fr. Daniel Berrigan

"NOTRE DAME students often encounter death for the first time during their college years. Many of our students have never been to a funeral. The death of a grandparent or a father or mother can be a moment of truth and a moment of anguish. The death of a Notre Dame student saddens the whole campus and can traumatize friends and roommates. The Notre Dame family never appears more genuine than at these times, when the people of Notre Dame rally to the support of those who mourn. We hope always to recognize one another at our own station of the cross—in this place, at this time."

—Nicholas Ayo, C.S.C., *Times of Grace*, 125.

"ONE NIGHT, while still a student, my mom called to tell me that my dad was very ill and that I better come home. Dad wasn't expected to live long.

"I was shaken. When I arrived at the hospital I found my family surrounding my Dad's bed. He was barely conscious but I could tell he recognized me. I felt helpless, but relieved and consoled that my family was gathered together. It was Holy Thursday. We read John's Last Supper discourses together as a family, and then slipped out and headed to Sacred Heart Church, to partake, as we had always done, in the liturgy of the Last Supper.

"Early the next day, Good Friday, we held hands and

prayed together, as my dad quietly slipped into uncon-sciousness, and then passed into eternal life. It was one of the defining moments of my life. As my dad lay before me lifeless, a central truth came crashing down upon me.--one that comes upon each of us at some level, when we are with someone as they die, especially if that person is close to us. If my dad died, then it was true that I would also die. Death is an experience that we all share in life. The question that posed itself was: If it is true that I will die, then how do I want to live"

—Fr. Timothy Scully, C.S.C, in *A Letter to My Freshman Self*, 204.

"THE LAST JUDGMENT will not be a day of wrath and reckoning, as we might conjecture in our vengeful, human imagination. Judgment Day will be an epiphany day. We will see the ways of God revealed. We will know how suffering was necessary to allow love to deepen. We will see how all the pieces of the jigsaw puzzle of this world's history do fit together to make the loveliest white rose, a vision of the Communion of Saints gathered together in Dante's visionary paradise beyond the stars. We shall see how every event or person that enters our life belongs to it and fits in the puzzle somewhere. We may be working with a corner of blue pieces and wonder what we will do with these red pieces. But they belong in the "Godscape" somehow and somewhere. We must wait for the revelation of love and for the epiphany of God. And when we see a gap in the pieces of our puzzled life, we must believe that the missing piece will be given to us. We will find the child lying in the manger that all along we have been seeking—the missing piece fulfilling the picture of God's love in this world."

—Nicholas Ayo, C.S.C., in *Times of Grace*, 68.

"I KNOW A RETIRED FRIEND who travels the backroads of the United States, mostly in summers, visiting small towns and trying to get a sense and flavor of the people who immigrated here over many years. One way he picks up this flavor of our history is by visiting cemeteries. On tombstones, he often finds epitaphs, some humorous, some serious, that give him a sense of how the relatives of the deceased thought of him or her. I'll quote just a few to give you a sense of it all. Sir John Strange: 'Here lies an honest lawyer and that it is Strange is no business of yours.' Or 'Here lies Lester Moore. Four slugs from a 44, no less, no more' And, 'On the 22nd, Jonathan Fiddle went out of tune.' Margaret Daniels: She always said her feet were killing her. Nobody believed her. Harry Edsel Smith: Born 1903–Died 1942. 'Looked up the elevator shaft to see if the car was on the way down. It was.' And 'Here lies an Atheist: All dressed up and nowhere to go.'

"So, why am I sharing all these epitaphs with you? First of all, they are pretty funny. Sometimes the lives of the deceased are rather humorous. Even death itself, when you think about it is sort of humorous. None of us wants to die, and yet we have no control over it. As a humorist once said, none of us will get off this planet alive.'

"Part of the reason I also wanted to share these poetic verses with you is that I have a sense that none of us wants to die and be unremembered. Our relatives and friends want us to be remembered. So they print mortuary cards or long obituaries. After all, it does seem to me that every person born onto this earth was important to somebody and, hence, should be recalled, remembered, spoken well of and written well of. Of course, the deceased person has no control over that, but someone else, someone living, has the option and they often make use of it.

"Epitaphs, obituaries and eulogies can give us a sense of the meaning of our own lives, its shortness and its tenuousness. In short, the lives of the dead are often a lesson for the living...The point that gives me some hope is the sense that we are all remembered. Life is precious. For many of us someone in this world will remember us after death, even if only on a grave marker. For all of us, our God will remember us."

—Fr.LeRoy Clementich, C.S.C., in *Seasons of the Spirit*, 123-25.

"HAVE YOU EVER had a resurrection experience? I obviously do not mean a rising from the grave, but something you could describe as life beginning all over again today. In other words, can resurrection be personal? I think we need to say that there is a difference between resurrection and immortality. Immortality simply means never dying. Resurrection, on the other hand, is a daily foretaste, a daily experience, something that is actually happening, something personal you could describe as worth getting up for in the morning. That's resurrection! So what are some examples of that? Well, have you ever known people of whom you could say that this person is always full of life, always happy, always hopeful, and always ready to find something good to say, even though things may not always go consistently well? That's a resurrection experience. Or have you ever personally had a bout with some sickness over a long period of time, perhaps even being confined to a hospital, and then finally being told by your doctor that you are cured, and healthy again and can go home. That's the feeling of resurrection. Or when two people, for instance, who dearly love each other but have had a falling out, decide to put their differences aside and love one another again—that's the experience of resurrection.

Are you moved by a smile on a child's face, a good joke, or some really humorous situation? That's resurrection Something has transformed your life and brought you happiness.

"The point of all this is to say that resurrection is happening all the time. It's going on at this very moment if we are aware enough to notice it, whether in ourselves or in the world around us.

Resurrection, in other words, is dynamic; you should be able to notice it when it is happening....

Easter is forever. And so are we."

Ibid.,152-3.

"FINALLY, we reach old age and we know that death is closer... Does not each one of us want to live forever or at least as long as we can, in case there is just one more possibility that could fill our heart's desire?

"The interesting and mysterious point in all this is that none of us really and ultimately understands what we are searching for. We do not understand our heart's desire; hence we keep searching throughout life, moving from one false start to another. I have often wondered if any of us will ever die fully happy, fully satisfied and convinced that we have realized our heart's desire.

"You may say: What has all this to do with love? Love seems to be that element in human life that directs us to something that will satisfy us and will give us full happiness and ultimate gratification. The huge dilemma, however, is this: the human soul is never satisfied. This temporary human object of my love will never be enough. The soul is always hungry for more, whatever 'more' is. I don't know if there is any solution to this longing, but my sense is that if we can manage throughout our life to direct our longing to the other, to that other person or cause—somehow imagining we can ultimately satisfy ourselves—perhaps that would be enough.

"I think this is why Jesus is such a beautiful example of this love. In his whole life, all he said, all he died for was done for us and for the whole human race. He had no selfish, personal intent. He lived and died for us—the other.

I am even confident enough to say that Jesus was probably the only person in world who died happily. Hanging on the cross, he had finally found his heart's desire.

"So then, weak as we humans are, distracted as we are by worldly desires, it might be well occasionally to ask ourselves whether this one achievement or this one moment in our personal history is what we are ultimately searching for and that which will provide fulfillment. My hunch is that we will probably go on wondering about all this until the Lord finally calls us to our heart's final desire, which is his kingdom where love is all there is."

—Fr. LeRoy Clementich, C.S.C., in *Seasons of the Spirit*, 208-09.

"AS THE JOURNEY IN LIFE enters the "home stretch," people find that so much of what was so very important becomes less urgent, pressing or vital. For so many years we seem to be "pulling" God into our lives, but near death the direction changes. It becomes God who now "pulls" us into eternal life beyond this world. In John's gospel Jesus promises, "…and, I, when I am lifted up from the earth, will draw all humankind to myself…In my Father's house are many rooms; if it were not so, would I have told you that I go to prepare a place for you? And when I go and prepare a place for you, I will come again and take you to myself, that where I am you may be also."

—Fr. Richard Berg, C.S.C., in *Fragments of Hope*, 132.

Packed for Heaven

"I KNOCK GENTLY on her door in the skilled nursing unit at Mary's Woods. Holy Names Sister Mary Jane is up in her chair today with her feet propped up on the box that serves as her footrest. Sister's eyes twinkle. She smiles. I ask, "What are you up to today?" She thinks I am referring to her weight loss as she is nearing the end of her life. "I really am not hungry, and I must weigh an ounce or two less than yesterday!" I smile. "Sister, I mean how are you doing?" "Well, I'm glad you asked. I'm doing fine. I'm getting packed for the trip home to God."

"We chat for awhile about her hospice experience and then she turns to the box at her feet. "Here, Father, I want to show you what I have packed." She opens the box and inside is her photo album. We look at pictures of her family, some Holy Names sisters, her friends, and a few students she taught over the years. "I love each and every one of them. That is what I'm taking home with me to God: my love for them. For a long time I've been planning and preparing for the future, for my trip home."

"Riding on the city bus one day the thought occurred to me that we should indeed plan and practice for going to heaven. That means practicing love. I was practicing for older age. Practicing for the years ahead was my Lenten resolution a few years earlier. So I resolved to get around using public transportation whenever possible. Tough at first, I soon came to enjoy the hours spent getting out to and back from Mary's Woods each day. Learning to use the bus brought a new freedom from traffic. I enjoyed moments to read, pray, prepare homilies and to nap. I also enjoyed being among the diverse and interesting community that uses public transportation.

"How to get ready and what to pack for our eternal change of address? Sister Mary Jane was so ready for her trip and so willing to teach. She knew her baggage was to be love, a deep love of God and love of others as herself. To her, heaven wasn't only about mansions in the sky; it was to be about being with loved ones, especially Jesus and Mary. With a life of devoted prayer and pictures of her loved ones in mind, she left Mary's Woods to spend eternity with her beloved God and beloved saints. She was so well prepared for her journey. She was well practiced for heaven.

"The day before Sister Mary Jane departed she and I blessed one another with the word of God: "Teacher," a scholar of the law inquired, "which is the great commandment in the law?" Jesus said to him, "You shall love the Lord your God with all your heart, and with all your soul, and with all your mind. This is the great and the first commandment. And a second is like it, You shall love your neighbor as yourself. On these two commandments depend all the law and the prophets."

"Our conversation then ended with a nod, the sacrament of anointing, a smile and the word "practice."

Faith includes hope for eternal life. We pray in the Lord's Prayer, "Thy will be done on earth as in heaven," and are led to practice for eternal life. We practice welcoming the Kingdom of God, hoping to draw God in our direction, thanking, praising, begging God's closeness, asking help for so many concerns. I often pray, "Please be here, Lord. I need your help, your inspiration, your healing...I trust your promises. Thank you for your remarkable promise as you departed from your disciples and ascended to heaven: 'I am with you always, to the close of the age.' Thank you for the gift of your Holy Spirit dwelling with us here and now."

"As the journey in life enters the 'home stretch,' people find that so much of what was so very important becomes less urgent, pressing or vital. For so many years we seem to be "pulling" God into our lives, but near death the direction changes. It becomes God who now "pulls" us into eternal life beyond this world. In John's gospel Jesus promises, "…and, I, when I am lifted up from the earth, will draw all humankind to myself… In my Father's house are many rooms; if it were not so, would I have told you that I go to prepare a place for you? And when I go and prepare a place for you, I will come again and take you to myself, that where I am you may be also."

—Fr. Richard Berg, C.S.C., in *Fragments of Hope*, 130-32.

ONE OF MY DEAREST FRIENDS, Professor Leroy Rouner, also a Methodist minister and editor of some 18 books for the University of Notre Dame Press, recounted the tragic loss of his 20 year old son in a mountain climbing accident. He wrote a book about it, *The Long Way Home.* The following is from pages of that book:

"The guy from Air India led me through turnstiles and waiting rooms and crowds of curious folk who turned to watch us as we hustled through, wondering what we were about, and then on the other side of a final barrier, there were Eric and Pat, strong and still and unsmiling.

I said, 'Eric, you have bad news.'

Eric said 'Yes.'

I said, What is it?'

He said, It's Timmy.'

I said, 'What happened?'

He said, He's dead.'

I said.'No!'

(I thought , 'Don't tell me that. Tell me it's Dad. I can cope with that. I know about that. That is something that is supposed to happen. Don't tell me it's Timmy.')

"I slumped against the wall and sank down on a bench. Pat knelt in front of me and Eric sat next to me with his arm around me, and I just kept saying 'No!' 'Shit!' and cried and twisted my body and my hands and my face, trying to get away from it, and escape and be free and have it not have happened, and get back to where I was before, when I didn't know, and there was still Timmy.

"Funny Tim, the long, gawky kid who knew how to take a joke. Timmy who cared about us all, and went to the National Training Laboratory psychology program and came home and tried to make a family out of two contentious parents. The Tim who came to my study in the evening to talk about his homework, and how the American Indians had the best values, and how we had to get back to that. The kid with the girlfriends, the kid who wrote poetry; the awkward one who seemed embarrassed when you hugged him but who was always the last one to let go..

"No, not Timmy, OK? Not Tim...

"I had never known about emptiness. Even when I was alone, I loved being alone. Loneliness was full of longing and hope. But now there was a dreadful fact that was never, ever going to be different. I couldn't believe it. I couldn't escape it. Nothing really bad had ever happened to me before, and things could always be made right somehow. If I broke a bone or wrote a bad term paper, or were mean to someone, I could let the bone heal, or rewrite the paper, or apologize for the meanness.

"I am more like my father than I had thought. He really couldn't remember having made an important mistake, but then, I couldn't remember having made a mistake I couldn't fix. 'Be ye therefore perfect as your Father in Heaven is perfect.' In our different ways, we both thought we had done that. But now I would never ever have Tim in my world again. A terrible thing had happened, and I couldn't do anything at all to fix it or make it right. So I wasn't perfect. I was empty and bereft. I was nothing, and Timmy's death was everything."

(and so, Leroy, his wife Rita and children, Rainsford, Jonathan and Tina, brought Tim's ashes home and held a wake for his family and friends and then had a service at St.Andrew's in Tamworth, New Hampshire... Leroy gave the sermon). This is what he said:

"Oh God of Grace and God of Glory, we open our grateful and grieving hearts to you
in thanksgiving for the life of our Timothy.
For the strength of his body and the keenness of his mind,

For the riches of his imagination and the awesome
tenderness of his spirit.
"We cherish dearly remembered times when he cheered
us with his wild sense of fun;
When he helped us with his sensitivity to feeling and
his fairness;
When he challenged us with new ideas and strong con-
victions;
When he loved us with that half-shy intensity
which bespoke so much integrity.
"We give you thanks, O Lord, for all this, and for all
those who helped Tim along life's way, and made life
such a blessing for him:
His teachers in school and college
His friends in India and here at home.
His mother who he adored
His younger brother and sister, whom he cherished,
His older brother, who was his best friend and boon
companion,
His larger family of grandparents, uncles, aunts and
cousins, in whose company he delighted.

"We give thanks especially for those who
taught him to ride, and to ski, and to climb;
Who taught him to love poetry and to think
well; and those who taught him the meaning of love.
"And we thank you too, Lord, for the beauty
of your earth, for all things bright and beautiful,
which were an inspiration for Tim and are
a healing balm for us: for rivers, and forests,
and those great high peaks of the Spirit which
Tim loved so well.

"We bless him to your infinite care and goodness,
confident that for him, and for us too,
'all shall be well, and all manner of things be well.'

…"And finally, O Lord, we pray for ourselves.
In your god time heal over the black hole in
our hearts, but bless us continually with the
memory of Tim's free spirit.

" 'Born of the sun, he traveled a short while
toward the sun,' and on his way blessed us
beyond measure.
For that great gift, O Lord, we praise your holy name.
Amen."

"I take new comfort from knowing that God's rain falls on the just and the unjust, and God's sun shines on the evil and the good. Timmy's death was not fair. That was really Bad News; But if God is not Lord of the Bad News as well as the Good, then he has no more power than our best human yearning for the Good. What I know about God's power is that he turned my mourning into thanksgiving; and in the life of the world to come, I believe he turns death into eternal life. I'm not quite sure what that means, but the power of an omnipotent God to save the world is a belief I cling to."

Leroy Rouner, in *The Long Way Home*, p. 105-06.

"NO ONE KNOWS how long we will be on this earth. Death will come to each person like a thief in the night. But for us children of God death is not something to be feared, as though it were a defeat or a total loss. No, death is truly our birth into eternal life with God. In faith, each of us can say with St. Paul that, from now on, 'a crown of glory awaits me.'

"I wonder if we spend enough time dreaming or fantasizing about heaven. St. Paul wrote that it hasn't so much as dawned on the human heart what God has waiting for those who love him. To me this sounds like a dare. It is as if he were saying 'Go on, dream big. Imagine the absolute best existence possible and you won't even come close to the blessedness of heaven.' The more we set out eyes on the kingdom of heaven, the better we will be able to live as true daughters and sons while here on earth.

"Still, Jesus know we might become anxious, or even preoccupied, with our death. That is why he said, 'Do not let your hearts be troubled' (jn:14:1). He will come back for each of us at an undetermined time. For our part we must live each day well in this joyful hope so that we will be ready for that great and glorious day."

—Fr. Bill Wack, C.S.C. in *Holy Cross, Our Only Hope.* Nov.14.

LIFE

*If you were charged in court
for being a Christian,
would there be enough evidence
to convict you?*

"THE POINT I WANT TO MAKE is that walking with God down every corridor, every day, means that you find a way explicitly to tie your identity to your faith so that you know who you are and what you stand for—and so does everybody else."

—Fr. Theodore Hesburgh, C.S.C., in
Walking With God in a Fragile World, 38.

A Prayer for Today

"TEACH ME to live a life that is better than mere existing

Teach me to love a person with more than wanting

Teach me how to clear my mind that is different from dis appearing

Teach me how to forgive myself in a way that does not grant me permission

Teach me how not to forget those I've lost that is not constant longing

Teach me to have passion that is not ruled by ruling

Teach me to give it away without ever expecting

Teach me to hear the silent whispers over constant rumbling

Teach me to be your servant, Lord with a pure heart and to desire nothing else."

"A SINGLE drop of water
is both wildly significant
and insignificant in all of the galaxies.
This drop of water is no more or no less
significant than the drop of water beside it.
Both are relatively powerless to the world at large.
It is not until the multitudes of droplets of water,
working together, becoming waves,
hurricanes, tidal waves, tsunamis and the like—
that they become forces of nature.
A single human is both wildly significant and
insignificant in all the galaxies. This
single human is no more or no less significant
than the human beside it.
Both are relatively powerless to the world at large.
But what if, like water, all the humans
pulled together and became their own force of nature?
My God, what would we have then?"

—Fee Thomas

"THE MENTALITY of the quick fix is one of the major
hindrances to happiness that our society engenders. We

do not like to postpone gratification: look at the national credit card debt. And we like to believe in the sudden conversion that promises to change hearts and correct wrongs quickly. Of course, real happiness, as distinguished from mere satisfaction, doesn't come easily. One clear day does not prove that spring is here; one good deed is not enough to make a person good—or happy. Expecting to change because the think we'd like to is the difference between wishing and willing. One is a dream and the other a hard choice knowingly made. It takes an unshakable resolution, built on something that is worth living for—and dying for—to command the daily practice necessary to build the virtues, the habits that make doing good our second nature. Like the repeated exercise that builds the body, repeated practice in necessary to train, employ and enjoy the passions according to the standard tells us is right and necessary. Virtue is not like a pet that comes obediently when called; it has a high price payable over a lifetime. The V chip cannot install virtue, nor can wishing make it ours.

"This is crucial because the concert of virtues, and only the concert of virtues, makes us free enough to be truly happy. The mind directs the concert. Like a maestro, it brings out the best of each instrument at its command and faithfully leads the overall movement to its perfect conclusion. The body, senses, emotions and wishes are put in the service of knowing truth and living with excellence, In the process they fulfill their own purpose while serving a higher one. Thus freed, the mind, which makes us human, is able to lead us to the highest plateau of human happiness.

"Given the price of admission, it is no wonder that scores of people have given up on happiness and settled for frequent, if temporary, gratification. Without hope and basic sustenance, the struggle for virtue becomes even more difficult. The seven deadly sins—pride, covetousness, lust, anger, gluttony, envy and sloth—daily offer their glittery invitation to taste the once forbidden fruit, though it is commonly no longer forbidden. Since we are all sinners, it is easy to take some delectation in the sins of others, particularly the famous or those whose offices formerly demanded respect, like our highest public officials, the clergy and those in the legal and medical professions....What is needed now is not political power, which is one of temptations Christ resisted in the desert, nor a safe shelter. Re need to recover, build and foster a spirituality that can live and grow in the midst of chaos, skepticism, and apparent absurdity. We need to rediscover the rock-hard truths of our Christian tradition and find in them fresh possibilities of life and grace.

"At the center of it all is the need to take the risks that lead to self discovery, growth and happiness. We need to remind ourselves that the Church Christ instituted was in the world as a pilgrim, not a landlord; as a teacher, not a dictator. It was a church of prophets who believed what they preached and so preached with an urgency that bore the stamp of saving conviction. The greatest defense of belief is to be found not in disputation, but in living and dying with moral courage. The sign by which the early Christians were recognized was 'see how they love one another.' And so it must be again. The Scriptures are about life in this world. The technologies ad complexities have changed since biblical times of course, but the truths and temptations haven't.

—Jim Langford, in *Happy Are They*, 6-7.

"THE GOSPEL and the teaching of Jesus reminds us constantly that we are always most properly judged in terms of our interior life rather than our public persona. In the end, the Christian paradox is that we are taught in the Gospel about the great reversal at the end of time, that those who are first in the world's eyes will be among the last and the last will be among the first. Those who are considered great in the Kingdom of God are those who have been the servants of the rest. At the end of one's life, it is not the fame that one has achieved or the economic success or political power, but rather the legacy of dedicated service that one leaved behind. Worldly success does not last forever and it is our responsibility to seek to make a positive difference in the world, especially in light of those who carry the heaviest burden during their earthly existence. The Christian paradox is ultimately a very positive message, for it gives all of us hope that, whatever our condition in life, we are beloved by God and that no set of temporary disadvantages can ever estrange us from the love and mercy of God."

—Fr. Monk Malloy, C.S.C., *in Monk's Musings*, 24.

GRAY, DREARY DAYS are part of nature's cycle. They are part of the human cycle also. We need those gray days in order to grow in holiness and wholeness. I would almost suspect that God builds in cycles of the 'blahs' because he knows this is the only way we'll grapple with the important questions. Blah times and depressions are truly a blessing.

Here I'm defining 'blessing' as anything that gets right to the center of your life and expands your capacity to love God, others and yourself. A blessing may not always be painless, but it will always bring growth!

One of the greatest blessings of sad days is that it forces us to look squarely at the question: Who am I? What is the meaning of my life? We're so used to defining ourselves by what we do. The valley days force us out of the normal routine of doing things. They take away our being-in-control, to remind us who we really are—creatures who are poor in spirit, totally dependent on our Creator for everything. We are given a chance to confront death, loneliness, change and to let go of the illusion of self sufficiency. Because of this letting go, we can turn toward God in expectation and trust, and experience his blessing. Remember Jesus' promise: 'Blessed are the poor in spirit, for theirs is the kingdom of heaven.'

"The gray days make us aware of time's passage and our aging. But the good news is that aging brings experience and wisdom. We mourn the passage of youth, but we can also rejoice in the new powers that come with growing in wisdom and age. Scattered ideas and values begin to come together, and we clearly see what it is that guides our lives. We can then affirm those values, or discard them for something newer, something that more reflects who we have become. Our lives begin to have substance, firmness, wholeness. I'm sure you will agree with me that your best growth as a person and as a Christian has taken place when you've passed through the fire and darkness of the valleys.

"The blah days are marvelous days for self knowledge., which is a prerequisite for fully loving God and neighbor. Psychologically speaking, depression is anger turned inward. So when you are aware of being depressed, ask yourself: What am I angry at? Who am I angry at? Is evil touching my life or am I just upset things aren't going according to my plans and desires? Depression is one of the ways your mind and body tell you that they are tired of running away from this or that, tired of your refusal or reluctance to resolve this issue or that unfinished business from the past.

"It is so exhausting to be cheerful all the time! Melancholy actually gives us time to recharge our batteries. One of the greatest mistakes we can make with people who are going through melancholy is to tell them to cheer up! They don't need that. They need the space, the solitude. They need to have their melancholy respected as a sacred time. Coldness, darkness and emptiness are as necessary to human growth as warmth, brightness, and fullness are.

"Many things can catapult you into the wilderness, or cause darkness to settle like a pall over your life. The death of a significant person, serious illness, rupture of a relationship, unemployment, the empty nest, retirement, a significant birthday, and new living situations are examples. You can be the victim of unjust accusations, or it can be the other way around: your sinful behavior finally backfires. A lessening of religious fervor can bring you to the desert, as can the inability to pray as you used to, or the sense of being abandoned by God, or apparently unanswered prayers. At other times, there seems to be no apparent reason why you find yourself in the wilderness. The desolation I can only attribute to the direct action of God.

"What is it like in the wilderness? It's not pleasant, that's for sure. There can be a loss of personal identity. You don't know who you are, or what the meaning and purpose of your life is. There is loneliness because you feel that no one else has ever experienced this before, and besides, all your usual props are are either crumbling or gone. You think about all the decisions and choices and you find yourself thinking: 'If only...' There is anxiety...Your whole being cries out to God and there is only silence...

"I write this as one who made it through the darkness and who survived the wilderness. There is light after, the Promised Land can be reached....I don't know how, where, or through whom God will deliver you, but what I do promise is that it will happen, if you don't run away from it, and if you remain faithful to a faithful God.."

—Fr. Herb Yost, C.S.C., *Waiting in Joyful Hope,* 125-6.

"SOMETIMES it really does help to change the perspective. Just by stepping to one side a tad we see things differently, and in the seeing, receive strength, wisdom, peace and encouragement—all signs of God's presence with us. I have a huge heating bill. Yes, but that means I have a home. Many don't. I have a huge pile of laundry to get done. Yes, but that means I have clothing. Many don't. I asked my teenage son to help clean the house. He's doing it but he is driving me nuts with his muttering. Yes, but that means he's not on the streets. I complain about taxes. Yes, they're heavy, but it means I have a job. It's a pain to find a parking spot close to the store entrance. Yes, I have to park further away, but it means I'm capable of walking and have been blessed with transportation. All my clothes are too snug, but that just means I have enough to eat. Yes, that alarm goes off in the morning and signals me to get up and start another yucky day. But it also means I'm alive....The heating bill, the whiney teenager, the pile of laundry, everything—are they the problem? Or are they signs of God's presence? God is where you are."

—Fr. Herb Yost,C.S.C., in *Waiting in Joyful Hope*, 78.

"There is a time to join,
a time to try, and a time to move on.
Each requires us to be attentive
and to be brave as we seek to find
and follow
the Spirit."

"IN NATURE, there are ceaseless cycles of activity and growth, followed by dormancy and hibernation. Activity must stop in order for new growth to happen We are part of the natural world, right? I'm not going to advocate hibernation, attractive as it sounds sometimes! But dormancy is another story. This is something you can do several times a day. Dormancy is Sabbath time. It's a brief moment in the day when you choose *not* to do something productive, so as to give your soul, mind and body a chance to take in nutrients so that you can remain productive. Push back from the desk, close your eyes for five minutes, and observe your breathing. Buy a rocking chair and sit in it regularly, not thinking, not praying, not talking to a friend, just sitting. Go some place where you just cannot be reached. Trust me, the world will get along without you for a few minutes. Dormant times make for a marvelous human being."

—Fr. Herb Yost, C.S.C. in *Waiting in Joyful Hope*, 155.

"NOISE CROWDS out silence as weeds crowd out flowers. There is no end to weeds, because a weed turns out to be whatever does not belong where something else is cultivated for beauty or for food. Noise is the weed of the sound world. It pops up, or blasts out, most everywhere. Lakes that once knew rowboats and sail boats now are drowned in the roar of jet-skis that whine in circles of spray and in one's face. There is no way one can broadcast silence. One can never take noise away with silence imposed on others, but noise imposed on others always takes away silence.

"Come dawn, quiet can be almost complete, as it seems noise must eventually sleep as well. One can find some silence around the campus lakes and amid the tall trees in the dell of ancient woods on the path along St. Joseph's Lake to the Calvary cross at the hilltop end of the outdoor Stations of the Cross. Those trees do not speak or take you into account. They do not expect you to talk to them or to listen to their story, though you can do so quietly. They broadcast only silence. Moments of silence without trucks, machines, airplanes overhead, or sirens in the distance do not occur at times. There are moments. On a New Year's Day, the university being closed, I walked the whole of the path around the God Quad as a gentle snow fell. There were only my footprints and there was no noise of any kind. People make noise, but there were no people but me, and my footfall was muffled by the blanket of deep and soft new-fallen snow. Silence is a plenum, and I imagine God living in an infinite silence that contains every word that could ever be spoken and then some. A white page, like a white snowfall, waits with infinite expectation for the first black scratch on its surface. Until one writes this and not that, the white page of silence stands in for the infinity of God, who contains all that is and all that could be. Eternal rest may be heaven's promise, but I hope there is no external noise before the face of God where a silence that is golden may well prevail."

—Nicholas Ayo, C.S.C. in *The Heart of Notre Dame*, p. 62-63

"FATHER HESBURGH emphasized that leadership involves articulating a vision and getting others to own it as their own, especially colleagues:

'The secret is really to get the best people you can get, even if they are better than you are, and to get them in the right slot. But once you get them appointed to that slot and get their agreement to do the work, then leave them alone. Don't try to second-guess them. Don't try to say who is going to be their assistant and who is going to work with them; that's their problem. I always told them "You do your work and I'll do mine. Whatever you do, you're going to get the credit for it, and whatever you do I'll back you on it. Unless you make an absolute mess of it, I'm with you all the way." As a result, people know they have their own balliwick that they are going to run themselves. They are going to pick their people and they are going to have a reasonable freedom to have their own particular vision within the larger vision.

Administrators who don't make it are fussy administrators who are constantly sticking their noses into other people's business and telling them how to do things. A much better system is to get people who know much more about a specific area than you do and let them go.'"

—Fr. Theodore Hesburgh, cited by
Robert Schmuhl in *Quotable Notre Dame*, 58

"WE CAN ALL LEARN something from the unexpected. We learn from the world around us as a child in fascination examining everything from the bug in the grass to the crack in the sidewalk. Alas, our spiritual sense of wonder, along with our bodily muscles, tends to atrophy as we age. We no longer read books to learn something new. We read to confirm what we have already concluded and now defend against change. We no longer look up words in the dictionary. We assume our vocabulary is sufficient and the author has chosen to obfuscate his or her writings with words seldom used and unnecessarily employed. In short, rather than learn from ever new and ever deeper experience, we impose our previously learned experience upon the present moment. We look for what we expect. And we do not expect to see ducks in the trees. We conclude that they are not normal. Indeed, they are queer ducks. They are not normal if what one means by normal the average waterfowl by statistical count. And yet they are wonderful and beautiful. The world is a better place because wood ducks create a variety and a form of beauty and behavior all their own. To see them with wonder-filled eyes is to see them as new and nothing to fear."

—Fr. Nicholas Ayo, C.S.C. in *Times of Grace*, 69-70.

WE CAN LIVE WITH HOPE even as we face life's fragility and our own contingency. I don't think God wants or needs us to suffer hunger, poverty, loneliness, discrimination or disease. Perhaps what God wants is for us to care for each other, nurture each other and work together to grow the economy of love in the world. God is love. As the song says, "Love is all you need."

To be anthropomorphic about it, if God cried, God's tears would drown the world. And if God smiled, we would not need the stars. But God does neither. Creation is God's mosaic and it cannot be completed until evil is vanquished by an abundance of good. In that sense, God does need us to add to the sum of goodness in the world

Sometimes this seems hopeless, surely a long shot. But if we help each other, if we walk with God, if we find and encourage the goodness in others, if we learn to serve, then we can cry for Him and smile for Him. We are His hands, His eyes, His heart on earth."

— Jim Langford, in *Walking with God in a Fragile World*, vi.

"People are capable of incredible kindness and decency—spontaneous, selfless, inexplicable goodness – the sort of kindness that just makes you shake your head and smile; kindness that seeks nothing in return and is its own reward. Try to be one of those people. There are many ways to take the measure of a life: dollars earned, awards won, miles logged, trophies bagged. I time you are going to realize that to the extent you were of use to strangers is as good a measuring stick as any. So go ahead--start now."

—Matt McGarry, in *A Letter to My Freshman Self,* 18.

"IF WE ALL BEGAN to walk more consciously with God in his world, the world would soon be less fragile. We cannot simply celebrate the spirit of volunteerism among the young. Each of us needs to find a way to help, no matter how full our daily time card already is. I cannot remember a time when I did not have a dozen things to do at once. As time went on, I learned how to give up the less important activities in order to do the important ones with full, undivided attention. I learned that you need not worry about what you just did; when you leave it, leave it. Don't worry about what you have to do tomorrow; there will be time enough for that tomorrow. Give the present your full attention.

"The real secret to meeting many demands is possessing inner peace. No matter what problems, pressures, or tensions, we will not be much good unless we think clearly and act calmly and resolutely.

"I truly believe that, with faith in God and in our fellow humans, we can together aim for the heights of human endeavor, and that we can reach them, too. Through all the miles and the moments of my walk, I have felt the presence of the One who is our creator and redeemer. What I hope my life might have to say, especially to the young, is this: He believed, he hoped, he tried, he failed often enough, but with God's grace he often accomplished more than he rationally could have dreamed. He gave witness to those wonderful words of Scripture: "God has chosen the weak of the world to confound the strong." So we are weak. No matter.

—Fr. Theodore Hesburgh, C.S.C.,
in *Walking With God in a Fragile World*, 44-45.

"WATCH and perceive. To go through life with eyes open for God, to see Christ in oppressed and unimportant people—that is what praying and watching is all about. We believe so that we can see, not so that we can shut our eyes to the world. We believe so that we can see—and can endure what we see.

If we want to sum up what watching and praying is about, we have to say: it is about an attentive life. Goodwill and helpfulness are fine, but they are not enough. Attentiveness is necessary, so that we can do the right thing at the right time in the right place.

"Live attentively: that means going into the new day, wholly present in mind, heart, and senses, in order to be present in that day with all our senses and all our powers, in the place where God is waiting for us."

—Jurgen Moltman, in *Walking with God in a Fragile World*, 70.

"WHAT YOU FOCUS on will multiply." That simple sentence has the power to change lives. Reflection confirms its truth. Think of small noises that annoy us. Once our attention is drawn to them, they seem to grow geometrically until we are unable to escape their intrusion. If we notice and focus on one small flaw, it will quickly take on a larger proportion and threaten to be all we see. One can park a new car at the extreme end of a mall lot and still come out to find that someone has put a small ding in the door. Once noticed, the ding becomes the focus of the owner's attention. It may not ruin the car, but it can surely ruin a day.

"On what do many of the forces in our lives in our lives—employer, the media, family members and friends or enemies—focus? If the focus is on the negative, the result will be an increase in fault-finding, fear, and a sense of futility. But if we see and focus on the positive aspects of things and people, if the news would tell good stories as well as bad, good things would multiply and so would our ability to visualize, plan and achieve them.

"We need to train ourselves to adjust our focus. We don't need to ignore problems or unpleasant realities, but we do need to see the potential for good; that will show us how to put the pieces back together in a new way."

"We tend to pigeonhole the various facets of our lives;

these are the things I have to do at home; these matters belong to my life at work; I cut the grass or go to the supermarket on Saturday. Sunday morning is for church. Of course we need to schedule our work to avoid chaos. But organization can also promote a mentality that sorts and separates things that should stay together.

"...The Christian life is a whole and entire way of life, not simply a list of truths or a set of rituals. It is an orientation and an outlook that never loses sight of the love of God and neighbor as our ultimate concerns—the goal and guiding post for all we do.

"Conversion, reconversion, and commitment are not about a day, an act, or a gift—they are about turning or returning one's whole being toward the good and enjoying the process and the results. This is not a somber way of life; it is a cause for happiness that God has invited us to the Great Banquet in the Kingdom and that we are able to bring our friends and neighbors and strangers along with us to the feast. However insurmountable the problems that face us, our society and the world, the reality of grace is strong enough to meet them. If we ask for this grace and let it point us in the right direction, it can and will touch the totality of all we are and do."

—Jim Langford, in *Happy Are They*, 139.

"LIFE IS FILLED with concerns. We prioritize them and try to attend best to those that matter most. At some point, each one of us has to attend to the top of the list, to the one that is the ultimate concern, the one that gives meaning, vitality and inspiration to all of the priorities below it. It is that choice—deciding what is most important in our lives—that determines how and where we will seek happiness.

—Jim Langford, in *Happy Are They*, 126,89.

Past The Gates Of Hell

"There comes a time when one must look away from
death and turn away from the dead; one must cling
to life, which is made of minutes, not necessarily
years, and surely not centuries; one must fight so as
not to be overwhelmed by history but to act upon it
concretely, simply, humanly. In the midst of national catastrophe, one must continue to teach and
study, bake and sell bread, plant trees and count
on the future.
One must not wait for the tragedy to end before
building or rebuilding; one must do it in the
very face of tragedy."

—Elie Wiesel, in *Five Biblical Portraits*, 105.

"SAGES AND PROPHETS do not preach the virtue of compassion because it sounds good; religious people are very pragmatic.

"All the great world faiths emphasize the importance of charity and loving-kindness because they work; they have been found to introduce us into a sacred realm of peace within ourselves. And they do that because they help us to transcend the demands of our insecure, greedy egotism that imprison us within our worst selves.

"St. Paul shows us how the practice of compassion deflates the ego. In his famous hymn to charity he explains:

'Love is always patient and kind; it is never jealous; love is never boastful or conceited; it is never rude or selfish; it does not take offense; and is not resentful. Love takes no pleasure in other people's sins, but delights in the truth; it is always ready to excuse, to trust, to hope, and to endure whatever comes' (1 Cor. 13:4–6). True religion has little to do with self-righteousness, which is often simply a self-congratulatory form of egotism. The discipline of compassion is the safest way to lay aside the selfishness and greed that hold us back from God and from our best selves.

"These are desperate times and the world seems a dangerous place. But for the vast majority of human beings, who are not fortunate enough to live in the First World, it has always been desperate and dangerous. Very few could dream of the security and power symbolized by the towers of the World Trade Center. Now we have joined the dispossessed, but instead of resenting this, we can see it as an opportunity to effect the spiritual revolution which alone can save our troubled world."

—Karen Armstrong, in *Walking with God in a Fragile World*, 120.

"SAVING FLESH at Ground Zero reveals that in laying hold of our vulnerability we lay hold of our strength. Reverence for human remains, heroic efforts to recover the lost, even the dread some workers feel as they face the day when they can no longer labor at the site, no longer keep vigil in the presence of victims, all of this testifies to the hope that claims a future. The future can only be ours, though, when we recognize that it belongs equally to everyone. The fragility of flesh known in the painful particularities of Ground Zero summons us to submit to its authority as a universal symbol. Only in its universality does it have power to save; only thus does it become the symbol the world cries out for, the symbol by which to gauge what is true and trustworthy amid the disintegration of worldly (and religious) structures of authority. The captivating force of the image of Ground Zero lies in the myriad manifestations of authentic human being evoked by conditions of shared human vulnerability. During the crisis of September 11 human beings instinctively risked taking responsibility for the voiceless victims remaining in the Pit. The future depends now upon our willingness to take responsibility for voiceless victims around the world. The vulnerability we have known is transformed into strength when we let it lead us into solidarity with the most vulnerable people of our world. The bonds forged among Americans in crisis must not end at our shores.

—Kathleen McManus, O.P. in
Walking With God in a Fragile World, 142.

"I DO NOT THINK you can become fully alive if you live in a black-and- white world. To be fully alive, you must be able to live in the gray. In a black-and-white world, success requires perfection, and the smallest missteps can spell certain disaster. A gray world comes with a safety net: mercy and forgiveness. This safety net makes it possible to fall and fail, but to get up again and again. This safety net makes it possible to trust in God's relentless mercy. You understand that you will fail, and you know that God will catch you. The safty net teaches us that mercy and grace are unmerited, free and abundant. Therese wrote that 'everything is grace.' The safety net helps us to understand this and that God can work through everything—good and bad—to bring about good.

"Being fully alive, I think, also requires a theology of abundance and generosity. There seem to be two theologies of life, one of abundance and generosity, the other of fear and scarcity. A theology of fear and scarcity means that we think that we're going to run out of mercy or love, or life or air. The apostles often operated out of fear and scarcity. *How will we ever feed all these people with so little?* And yet we know that their fear was unfounded. In the story of the Loaves and Fishes, not only did they feed the 5,000 members of the gathered crowd, they had more left afterwards than they had when they started!

"The whole world is oriented toward a theology of abundance and generosity. It takes one seed to start a tree and yet millions of seeds fall. This theology of abundance and generosity invites us to give ourselves over to life, to live, to give ourselves, to spend ourselves, to burn out rather than rusting out. A theology of abundance and generosity allows us to fall and to get up, to trust in God's work in our lives and not in our accomplishments.

"A wonderful paragraph in the book *The Shoes of the Fisherman* by Morris West reads:

> 'It costs so much to be a full human being that there are very few who have the enlightenment or the courage to pay the price...On has to abandon altogether the search for security, and reach out to the risk of living with both arms. One has to embrace the world like a lover, and yet demand no easy return of love. One has to accept pain as a condition of existence. One has to count doubt and darkness as the cost of knowing. One needs a will stubborn in conflict, but apt always to the total acceptance of every consequence of living and dying.'

"This quotation speaks of a theology of abundance and generosity, a theology of a safety net of mercy and forgiveness. My heart breaks for people who do not have this safety net. Without this safety net, they have to live in a black-and-white world, no room for failure and growth, no room for dying and rising, and little room for mercy and forgiveness, making it virtually impossible to become a full human being.

"If becoming fully alive means Christ being my life, my all, my everything, then we all want it desperately. But we can only get there with a safety net of mercy and forgiveness, with a theology of abundance and generosity. In that abundance and generosity, we are open to the relentless mercy of God, which saves us at every moment of our existence. Being fully alive gives wonderful glory to God, or, as St. Irenaeus put it, is the glory of God. May we all aspire to such a glorious way of living."

—Fr. Joseph Corpora, C.S.C., in *Being Mercy*, p.2-4

"IN OUR LIVES, filled with clutter and chatter, with unfinished business and rough edges, with cell phones and bitmojis, it often seems we have no room at the inn. We barely keep ahead of the day's demands and messiness, all of which is necessarily gray. God is not waiting for our lives to be pure light, pure white, pure virtue so he can be born into them. Rather, as James Finley says, "God is being born, unexplainably born, in our hearts moment by moment, breath by breath." We find him in the "interior richness of every living thing that happens to us and everyone around us."

Why are we so afraid if gray? Why do we strive for black and white when we know things aren't that way?

'

Maybe it's because we want to live with certitude. Yet, when certitude lessens the need for faith it can be a problem.

"As I get older the only thing I am sure of—or at least as certain as a person can be in this life—is the mercy of God. No one stands outside the embrace of God's mercy. It is available to all of us, as we are, where we are, how we are."

—Fr. Joe Corpora, in *Being Mercy*, 40 .

"TO LAUGH OFTEN and much, to win the respect of intelligent people and the affection of children, to appreciate beauty and find the best in others, to leave te world a bit better, whether by a healthy child or a garden patch—to know even one life has breathed easier because you have lived. This is to have succeeded!"

—Ralph Waldo Emerson

The Grotto

"Every University has a place where students hang out for their social life, libraries where they study, and playing fields where they play sports, but how many have a praying place?"

—Fr. Theodore Hesburgh, C.S.C.

"THERE ARE MANY PLACES on campus that are important to students. While students have special connections with their dorms, favorite classroom buildings, study spaces, or dining halls, all Notre Dame students have an affinity for The Grotto, making it one of the most sacred and beloved places on campus.

"Tucked away behind the Basilica and facing out towards St. Mary's Lake, The Grotto is far from being the most prominent or central location on campus. Built with rocks and adorned with candles and statues, there is nothing immensely impressive about The Grotto. But as the Stadium is loved for its traditions and grandiosity, and the Dome for being an icon, The Grotto is beloved because of its tranquility and simplicity.

"There are no ancillary usages or purposes of The Grotto. No statues mix religious iconography with that of football. No traditions of shotgunning beers or trying to hook up. Notre Dame Students use it for prayer, and, unlike other places around campus, this prayer is not to prove how religious they are, but just because they want or need to pray.

"The Grotto is the place where Students go when they most need it, or when they don't need it at all. They go there when they are feeling homesick. They go there when a relative is sick or has died. They go there when they have lost their way. Some students go there regularly to pray, while other students go there more infrequently. All spend at least a little time there over the course of their four years to think in silent reflection and maybe light a candle (although they rarely leave an offering for said candle, see #3).

"Notre Dame Students love The Grotto not only because of its beauty or history, but because it is there for them when they need it most. They love The Grotto because it is theirs, and they love The Grotto because it is truly unique to Notre Dame."

—B. Kessler, in *Things Notre Dame Students Like*, 40.

"I HAVE BEEN here{at Notre Dame) long enough now to have seen a lot of the place, to have been disappointed in its human frailties, to have moved far beyond the rosy patina of memory, romance and sentiment. But when I have become disillusioned or grumpy, when I have witnessed too much of the politics and personalities, I take a walk And the campus, the very place itself welcomes me as it did so many years ago. I have only to walk the lakes or sit alone at the Grotto or rest on a bench and watch a while in order for the place to show itself again, to reside in me, to work its spell again. And I know that there is something here, the landscape itself, that transcends the human, that sustains the promise and the legacy, that suggests the smile of God."

—Kerry Temple, in *Quotable Notre Dame*, 167.

"HOW IS GOD better glorified than by intelligent and devoted service to others in the line of our life's work? Neither God nor mankind is well served by mediocrity."

—Fr. Theodore Hesburgh, C.S.C.,in *Quotable Notre Dame*,126.

"WE HAVE ALL been gifts from the Lord. The first thing I must do is identify them. Then we must put them in the service of God and of one another.

"Investing our gifts in the service of others is a risk—but it is a risk that we must take. Success on a risk is not important. What is important is the freedom that comes from risking.

'In the Parable of the Talents (Matthew 25:14-30)

Jesus severely criticizes the servant who congratulated himself for not risking his master's money. Jesus opposes fear. The one who refused to invest the talents he was given because he was selfish. He failed to invest because he was afraid. Fear keeps us from being truly alive and from sharing the gifts that God has given us. We cannot listen to those voices of fear. Fear is often the first cousin of sin.

"Our gifts are not given us to be put in a safe, But to be spread, to be given, to be offered. Imagine all the mercy and forgiveness God has given you. What good is it if you lock it away in a safe? No! Give it away freely and generously. God will increase it....We are all called on to take a risk on the talents God has given us. In his mercy, he will be faithful to us."

—Fr. Joe Corpora, C.S.C., in *Being Mercy*, 75-76.

"IT'S HARD TO BELIEVE, isn't it? But it's true. We are God's delight! There are two things we celebrate at Christmas. One is, of course, the entry of God into human history through his birth as a human being. But we also celebrate ourselves. God has embraced us totally, completely, without reservation or conditions. The Good

News of Christmas is that we have a God who freely chose to live the life we live. The beauty of Christmas is the fact that it gives you and me reason to walk tall, to walk proudly and confidently on this earth. God glories in us. This is the real tidings of joy announced by the angels!

"So this Christmas, use your imagination and wrap yourself up in imaginary gift wrapping, the brighter the better! Or, for real, take one of those great big bows that has that sticky piece of cardboard on the bottom and stick it on your forehead! And then say: 'Here I am, Lord. You gave yourself to me. You said that you delight in me. So here I am, with all my goodness and warts, with my joys and my sadness, with things I do like about me and things I do not.' And I believe God will react just like any wide-eyed child when they see the tree and the gifts on Christmas morning! Listen to the Sunday Advent Scriptures. They tell us what God thinks of us. If you have trouble believing in your goodness, touch the lives of others with your warmth. Then, for all of us, Christmas will truly be a day of rejoicing everyday, and for the fullness of the Lord's coming we will all be waiting with joyful hope."

—Fr. Herb Yost, C.S.C., in *Waiting in Joyful Hope*, 227.

Suffering Should Never be Wasted.

"FATHER JIM WILLING, a beloved priest from Cincinnati, Ohio, suffered excruciating pain as he battled cancer. Though Fr. Jim eventually succumbed to the disease, his unconquerable spirit continues to uplift others bearing through their illness. The following excerpts from his book, *Lessons from the School of Suffering* speak to our Lord's promise that 'Your sorrow will turn into joy.' Fr. Jim gives us insights for bringing meaning to our suffering, dealing with our demons, helping another when words fail, and taking the long view on suffering.

"What I want to say to every suffering person is that suffering should never be wasted. Never. The worst thing that could happen to us is not that we would suffer, but that we would waste our suffering or simply endure it. Instead, we should grow from it, and learn from it, and let us unite us to the Lord.

"'We all have our "demons" or hurts that regularly trip us up...the demon is anything that "demeans" or hurts us or others in any way...they seem to wait to attack, like enemies at battle, in our weakest times, when we are least able to fight back. It is helpful to realize how our demons have power over us. Therefore we need to know what to do or where to go for help."

—Kathy Sullivan, in *I Had Lunch with God*, 112.

136

Sin:

"...SIN is always a sign of inadequacy. It is always a symptom that points to an insufficiency of love. As the Old Testament revealed in its simple wisdom, sin is the missing of the mark, the failure to measure up. It is always the absence of something: the failure to love when love is needed, the failure to respond when someone is in want, the failure to be true when fidelity had been my pledge, the failure to take a stand when a decision is demanded, the failure to act, to care, to forgive, to understand, to be merciful, to be compassionate.

"When we refer to Jesus taking away 'the sins of the world,' we mean He takes away our inadequacy, our insufficiency. Thus it's not so much a question of taking away as it is of adding something, bringing something to us—namely, the saving presence of the Father.

"I am thoroughly convinced that only at this point of understanding does the sacrament of penance make sense. I don't bring my toothache to the dentist, I bring my tooth. The pain of the toothache does me a favor: it is a signal indicating how much I need to seek out the dentist. By the same token, I don't bring my sin to the confessional, I bring myself, the sinner. The recognition of my sinfulness helps me realize how important it is for me to seek out the Lord, revealing and opening myself so that He, who alone can heal my inadequacy, can work His miracle within me."

—Fr. Bill Toohey,C.S.C., in *Life After Birth*, 97-98.

"I BELIEVED then, as I do now, that religion and spirituality are fed, not obstructed, by humor. They no not require being somber. Holiness should lead to smiles, not to sanctimonious observances. Law and rules are necessary, but too much focus on the letter of the law can squelch the spirit and block the happiness of the soul."

—Jim Langford.

"YOU ARE NOT CALLED to be Mother Teresa. You have to give you. You have to discover what the best, richest, wisest way to give yourself is in your circumstances... because the world has never had you. And it does need you or God would not have made you."

—Fr. Michael Himes.

"Though much is taken, much abides; and though
We are not now that strength which in old days
Moved earth and heaven, that which we are, we are;
One equal temper of heroic hearts,
Made weak by time and fate, but strong in will
To strive, to seek, to find, and not to yield."

—Tennyson

NO MATTER HOW BLEAK it seems at times, no matter how chance and circumstances have blindsided us, we need to grab every glimmer of hope and resolve to fight on. Suffering is part of every life; we cannot cure it, but we can overcome it. Rely on others and let them rely on you. The answer is in large part outside ourselves; we need to seek it for ourselves or be it for others.

The merciful person has a heart for those in need. Working on their behalf comes not from superiority, pity or munificence. It comes simply from love.

We are all part of the human race; we are part of each other. The implications of that truth could radically change how we view each other, regardless of skin color, culture, status or beliefs. This is not to say that all things are relative, but it is to say that all things are related.

"In the long run, what really matters is who and what you loved, the example you set for others, the way you accepted the good and not good in your life. And, above all, the grace that God sent through you to those who needed your embrace, your words, your inspiration...and your love."

—Jim Langford

" 'I THIRST'—words from the Cross; words heard in the midst of drought-stricken lands, in the poverty of inner cities, in the midst of wars. 'I thirst'—words of spiritual emptiness heard in urban centers, in green groves, and on barren plains. Perhaps our greatest challenge is to find the deep wells of physical and spiritual nourishment that will slake the thirst of a wounded and weary world."

—Grover Zinn, in *Echoes From Calvary*, p. 125

"HAPPINESS in this life is precious precisely because it is part of a dynamic process and therefore both fragile and fleeting. But we know something of ultimate happiness through our experience of joy in this world. Good and joyful things will provide a glimpse of what it will be like where true joy is to be found in our final reunion with God."

—Leroy Rouner, in *The Pursuit of Happiness*, p.3

Happiness

"THE GOSPEL of St. Matthew points an unambiguous and eloquent portrait of the kind of people who will be invited into the kingdom of heaven:

'For I was hungry and you gave me food, I was thirsty and you gave me something to drink, I was a stranger and you welcomed me, I was naked and you gave me clothing, I was sick and you took care of me, I was in prison and you visited me. Then the righteous will answer him, 'Lord, when was it that we saw you hungry and gave you food, and thirsty and gave you something to drink? And when was it that we saw you a stranger and welcomed you, or naked and gave you clothing? And when was it that we saw you sick and in prison and visited you?' And the king will answer them, Truly, I tell you, just as you did it to one of the least of these who are members of my family, you did it to me.' "(25:35-40)

"In every life there are conflicts, great and small, that threaten to shrink our souls and narrow our gaze with anger and hate, envy and pride. When well being is lacking, violence is sure to follow. For there to be peace, there must first be care and respect, and opportunity and empowerment and the freedom to choose responsibly. In Christian terms, there must be a "yes" to the offer of grace.

"'Happy the meek, for they will inherit the earth.' 'Meek' does not mean timid or indecisive, weak or passive. Only the strong can be meek; only those who have some mastery over themselves can be truly gentle to others. And that's what meekness is: it is being a gentle person. It is discovering and building power within oneself so that one can approach others with respect rather than status as the guiding principle of interaction. What an incredibly different society we would have if spouses, parents, employers, teachers, clerks, car drivers, civil servants—in fact everyone—concentrated on building inner strength so that civility and gentleness could replace crudeness and power games as the expected and accepted manner of our interactions with one another.

"It is not always clear what "satisfied" means in the beatitude "Happy are they who hunger and thirst for what is right, for they shall be satisfied..." People who are consumed by hunger and thirst for what is right never seem to be satisfied. It is as though the only response they can give to the invitation of Jesus, "Come to me all of you who are weary and I will give you rest" is OK but wait a minute..."So long as there are people with no shelter or food, people who are shriveled with loneliness, people who are abandoned or abandon themselves to a subhuman existence, the work is unfinished and they are unable to rest. There is more to be done, more they must do.

"These are not people deluded into some kind of savior complex that makes them think they are indispensable in the process of saving the world. But is simply that their whole being burns with a passion that cannot be lessened without altering their deepest understanding of themselves. To have that passion is to always to have a hunger and thirst that is never completely filled or quenched. They are people driven by love to go wherever it leads them: to the poor, the powerless, the handicapped and disabled, the sick and lonely, the young, the aged. They know that the coldness of indifference, the offering of hollow excuses and the burden of unfairness will always be with us as surely as pain and poverty will. But, like Sisyphus repeatedly pushing the rock up the mountain, knowing full well that it will fall back down just as he is about to reach the top, and that he will go down and start over, these people in their doggedness are the ones who fuel the eternal fame of hope.

"What a blessing it is to feel so deeply, to care so intensely. Surely a smile or a simple 'thank you' from someone they have helped brings a genuine reward. There must be satisfaction in standing up for those who cannot defend themselves, some reward in this life for those who refuse to leave the wounded behind. Happiness, after all, comes to be and grow only on the completion of a mission; it is born in the doing itself.

In the kingdom of heaven, God will reveal the perfection of the two virtues most exemplified by those who hunger and thirst for what is right. In God's kingdom there is both justice and mercy.

"I have found that the face of happiness is the face of someone surprised by your care, given a glimmer of hope by your help, made to sense their own worth by your affirmation, empowered to change themselves and others because you reminded them of their dignity. The face of happiness is the face of a child able to smile. A child's smile can light up a whole room. The power is such that the smiles of many could remake the world. Really. As a child Jesus amazed the elders at the Temple with his wisdom. As an adult, he welcomed the children over the protests of his disciples who wanted him to rest. In fact, he insisted that only those who become like little children will be saved. It is a gift of nature that, as we age, we we return to the simplicity of childhood.

"The Christian life is a whole and entire way of life, not simply a list of truths or a set of rituals. It is an orientation and an outlook that never loses sight of the love of God and neighbor as our ultimate concern –the goal and guiding post for all we do.

"Conversion, reconversion and commitments are not about a day, an action, or a gift—they are about turning or returning one's whole being toward the good, and enjoying the process and results. This is not a somber way of life; it is a cause for happiness that God has invited us to the Great Banquet in the kingdom and that we are able to bring our friends and neighbors and strangers along with us to the feast. However insurountable the problems that face us seem, our society and the world, the reality of grace is strong enough to meet them. If we ask for it and let it point us in the right direction, it can touch the reality of all we are and all we do".

—Jim Langford

"The saints are sinners who kept trying."

—Robert Louis Stevenson

"ARISTOTLE built an entire ethics on an understanding that the ultimate goal of human life is happiness. Because we can know and love, he reasoned, we are obligated to search until we find whatever constitutes true happiness and then to seek it with all our might...

"Without question, the imposters that promise happiness are powerful and they play to our weaknesses constantly and with unfailing attraction. Seven hundred years ago St. Thomas Aquinas admired their seductiveness even as he pinpointed the limitations that mark them as pretenders...What comprises the complete good? Some say wealth or pleasure of the senses; others see power, fame or honors as deserving of their ultimate concern. Aquinas argued that the goods we find in the world can truly be wonderful, but that not one, nor even all combined can exhaust our desire to know and love without limit. Limitlessness is the key. Created things, hemmed in by finitude and fragility, cannot guarantee more than a participation in happiness, a taste of what unbounded happiness might be like. And that taste serves only to whet our appetites for more. St. Augustine who personally tried every possible source of happiness, concluded that only God will do: 'You have made us for yourself and our hearts are restless until they find their rest in you.'

"But incomplete and limited as they are, money, sex, power and drugs continue to lure us, and we continue to succumb. Perhaps this explains why we are so angry. If we mortgage our spirit and barter away our self respect, and the end result is never enough, never enduring, we are forced to give up what remains of our dwindling souls to try for more. Without admitting it, we know we have been swindled. Endlessly. Willingly."

—Jim Langford, in *Happy Are They*, 2-3

"I WANT TO BE REAL CLEAR about something: when folks talk about "lazy panhandlers" you are talking about me. Yes, in my darkest and most humiliating days that was me with the sign. But God is good and I rose. I became a youth worker for at risk youth because I knew what it was like to be a "throw away kid". And now I write poetry for books in all parts of the globe. Not my doing, His grace. His grace that I'm even alive. So before you generalize those who have to stand out in front of people and beg think of your worst day and imagine it being in public. Think of me, because I AM MY BROTHER. And SO ARE YOU."

—Fee Thomas

PRAYER

"THE DIFFICULTY centers around the so called prayer of petition. Jesus seems to encourage our asking for things. He explicitly says 'Ask and it will be given to you, search and you will find, knock and the door will be opened to you.' Well, we've done this loads of times and it hasn't worked. What is this, a cruel game God plays with us? We have engaged in prayer time and time again, but more often than not, we haven't received any answer to our asking, searching, knocking.

"...We may suppose we are expected to wear God down with a dogged persistence (something like a salesman making his pitch to a tough-to-sell client). We sense there's something wrong in this, however. We don't feel attracted to a God for whom we have to fulfill predetermined commands before He will respond. That contradicts the God Jesus reveals.

"The fact is this interpretation twists things completely. The idea is not our trying to get through to God, but His attempting to get through to us. We may be inclined to think that prayer 'is our working on God,' but it is just the opposite. It works on us, opens us to the pursuing God.

"Prayer is our answer, not God's. He pursues us and constantly would afford us an experience of His loving presence…We see that we need to persist, not because God is hard to reach, but because we are. We need to persist in our efforts to listen, to open our hearts and reply to His call"

—Fr. Bill Toohey, C.S.C., in *Life after Birth*, 70-71.

"THERE IS, within this place called Notre Dame, some ineffable presence, a spirit, a soul that permeates the physical, tangible reality of campus. A touch of the divine dwells here. And I feel it, I think, because that quiet, mysterious presence resonates with something deep inside us—some other ineffable presence, spirit or soul that responds to this sacred and very special place. I felt it when I first came here, and I have felt it through the years—the realization that here there is no barrier, no division between the physical world we know through our five senses and the spirituality we know in our heart. Notre Dame, in its very landscape and architecture and geography, is infused with and animated by this holy moment. And those open to its touch are blessed by its stunning emission of grace."

—Kerry Temple, in *Celebrating Notre Dame*, 6.

"ONE OF the results of active engagement with the world is the need to grapple with the full mystery of the human condition—to account for both sins and grace. This requires a kind of self-awareness by each member of our university community about his or her potential for good or evil and a regular assessment of the structures of the common life to determine whether they foster or deter our common life and our mutual obligation to one another.

"But the realities of sin and grace are not simply pertinent to the internal life of themselves institution; they also help us to ponder how to keep hope alive in a world too often tempted to despair and cynicism. It s one of the great temptations of the modern academy to stand on the sidelines of history satisfied with occasional ironic utterances of glib put downs directed at power brokers of the political, economic, and social spheres. A much better alternative is to try to produce thoughtful leaders, informed prophetic voices, and people of integrity and good sense."

—President Emeritus Fr. Monk Malloy, C.S.C.,
in *The Spirit of Notre Dame*, 3.

"WE NEED to shine our light of invitation as brightly as possible, aiming it squarely into the darkest recesses of ignorance or hopelessness. We need to cultivate the gifts that this spirit of Notre Dame gives us, and we need to treasure and celebrate the fruits. And then we need to do what Notre Dame does best—go out and share stories about the relationships, the lessons, the places and the legacies that still call out to pilgrims like us."

—President Fr. John Jenkins, C.S.C.
in *The Spirit of Notre Dame*, 264.

Bibliography

Anderson, Terry. *Den of Lions*. New York: Random House, 1993.

Ayo, Nicholas, *The Heart of Notre Dame*, Notre Dame, IN: Corby Books, 2009.

Signs of Grace, Lanham, MD: Rowman and Littlefield, 2001.

Times of Grace, Lanham, MD: Rowman and Littlefield, 2004.

Your God May Be Too Small, Notre Dame, IN: Corby Books, 2014.

Berg, Richard, *Fragments of Hope*, Notre Dame, IN: Corby Books, 2011.

Corpora, Joseph, *The Relentless Mercy of God*, Notre Dame, IN: Corby Books, 2017.

Being Mercy, Notre Dame, IN: Corby Books, 2019.

Doing Mercy, Notre Dame, IN: Corby Books, 2020.

Clementich, Leroy, *Seasons of the Spirit,* Notre Dame, IN: Corby Books, 20011.

Gawrych, Andrew and Grove, Kevin, *The Cross, Our Only Hope,* Notre Dame, IN: Ave Maria Press,2008.

Griffin, Robert, *In The Kingdom of the Lonely God,* Lanham, MD: Rowman and Littlefield: 2003.

Kang, Lily and Ian Tembe, *A Letter to My Freshman Self,* Notre Dame, IN: Corby Books, 2016.

Kaplan, *Abraham, Love...and Death,* Ann Arbor: U. of Michigan Press, 1973.

Kempf, Haley, E. Boyle &M Bulgarelli, *A Letter to My Freshman Self,* Vol. 2, Notre Dame, IN: Corby Books, 2018.

Kennedy, Joseph, in *Go Forth and Do Good,* Notre Dame, IN: U.of Notre Dame Press, 2003.

King, James, *Known by Name,* Notre Dame, IN: Corby Books, 2008

Langford, Jeremy, *God Moments,* Maryknoll, NY: Orbis Books, 2001.

Langford, Jim, *Happy Are They,* Ligouri, Mo: Triumph Books, 1997.

Walking with God in a Fragile World: Notre Dame, IN: Corby Books, 2013.

Quotable Notre Dame, Notre Dame, IN: Corby Books, 2011.

The Times of My Life, Notre Dame, IN: Corby Books, 2015.

Malloy, Edward "Monk," *Monk's Musings*, Notre Dame, IN: Corby Books, 2015.

McBrien, Richard, *Catholicism*, Minneapolis: Winston Press, 1980.

Mooney, Christopher, *Teilhard de Chardin and the Mystery of Christ*, N.Y.: Doubleday, 1968.

Rouner, Leroy, *The Long Way Home*, South Bend: Diamond, 1989.

Loneliness, Notre Dame: U.of Notre Dame Press, 1998

In Pursuit of Happiness, Notre Dame: U. of Notre Dame Press, 1995

Kathy Sullivan, *I Had Lunch with God*, Notre Dame, IN: Corby Books, 2008.

Thomas, Fee, *Dreams Don't Die*, Notre Dame, IN: Corby Books, 2020.

William Toohey, *Life After Birth*, Notre Dame, IN: Corby Books, 2003.

Fully Alive, St. Meinrad, IN: Abbey Press, 1976.

A Passion for the Possible, Notre Dame, IN: Ave Maria Press, 1972.

Yost, Herb, *Waiting in Joyful Hope*, Notre Dame,IN: Corby Books,

p. 64